D1408646

# GLOBAL ORGANIZATIONS

## The European Union

# GLOBAL ORGANIZATIONS

The African Union

The Arab League

The Association of Southeast Asian Nations

The Caribbean Community and Common Market

The European Union

The International Atomic Energy Agency

The Organization of American States

The Organization of Petroleum
Exporting Countries

The United Nations

The United Nations Children's Fund

The World Bank and
the International Monetary Fund

The World Health Organization

The World Trade Organization

# GLOBAL ORGANIZATIONS

# The European Union

Peggy Kahn
University of Michigan–Flint

**CHELSEA HOUSE**
PUBLISHERS
An imprint of Infobase Publishing

090290

DOVER FREE PUBLIC LIBRARY
32 EAST CLINTON ST.
DOVER, NJ 07801

**The European Union**

Copyright © 2008 by Infobase Publishing

All rights reserved. No part of this book may be reproduced or utilized in any form or by any means, electronic or mechanical, including photocopying, recording, or by any information storage or retrieval systems, without permission in writing from the publisher. For information contact:

Chelsea House
An imprint of Infobase Publishing
132 West 31st Street
New York NY 10001

**Library of Congress Cataloging-in-Publication Data**
Kahn, Peggy, 1953-
  The European Union / Peggy Kahn.
    p. cm. — (Global organizations)
  Includes bibliographical references and index.
  ISBN-13: 978-0-7910-9538-6 (hardcover)
  ISBN-10: 0-7910-9538-X (hardcover)
  1. European Union. I. Title. II. Series.

JN30.K34 2008
341.242'2—dc22          2007042706

Chelsea House books are available at special discounts when purchased in bulk quantities for businesses, associations, institutions, or sales promotions. Please call our Special Sales Department in New York at (212) 967-8800 or (800) 322-8755.

You can find Chelsea House on the World Wide Web at http://www.chelseahouse.com

Series design by Erik Lindstrom
Cover design by Ben Peterson

Printed in the United States of America

Bang FOF 10 9 8 7 6 5 4 3 2 1

This book is printed on acid-free paper.

All links and Web addresses were checked and verified to be correct at the time of publication. Because of the dynamic nature of the Web, some addresses and links may have changed since publication and may no longer be valid.

# CONTENTS

# INTRODUCTION

# David and the European Union

DAVID, 14, LIVES WITH HIS PARENTS IN ISLINGTON, A DISTRICT of London. London, the United Kingdom's capital city and a world center of business, culture, and politics, has a population of about 7.5 million people. The United Kingdom, also called Great Britain or the U.K., is a wealthy country in Europe, with a democratic government.

Islington has a high population density—people live close together—and a total population of about 175,000. David's house, built in 1779, is five stories tall, has two rooms on each floor, and is in a row of five houses that touch each other. On the busy streets, you can see not only white and black Britons but also people who have recently come from Africa, the Caribbean region, and Bangladesh in southern Asia. While there are many well-off people and good restaurants with food from all over the world in Islington, there are also many poor families.

The U.K. government is not the only government making laws that affect David and his family. The United Kingdom joined the European Union (EU), now an organization of 27 countries, in 1973, 18 years after it was first established by the Treaty of Rome. The European Union also makes laws that affect David and his family.

## WHAT DAVID THINKS ABOUT THE EUROPEAN UNION

David strongly supports the idea of the EU, a system of decision making and lawmaking in addition to, and in many cases above, that of his country. He explains that the realities of modern Europe mean that governments cannot just go their own way but need to work together closely. Businesses operate and compete across countries; people move around for work, study, and leisure; and air and water pollution cross borders. David also says that embracing Europe fully would make England more of a democracy, because part of being a democracy means working with and negotiating with your neighbors. Many of David's friends, as well as leaders and other people in the United Kingdom, disagree. They say the EU undermines Britain's ability to make its own laws for its own people. Critics say that, while it may be difficult for ordinary people to influence British politics, it is almost impossible to participate in EU decision making.

Some Britons argue that becoming European "undermines British culture," but David thinks that there are some aspects of British culture that should be undermined—bad behavior at soccer games, the existence of a royal family in a modern, democratic country, and the tendency not to know what is happening in other parts of Europe and the world. David thinks of himself equally as British and as European.

The EU tries to remove barriers to trade between European countries and create a single economy in Europe. David has some doubts about whether free trade and market competition in a Europe-wide economy are always good for everyone, but he thinks that on the whole making Europe one big economy is a good idea. A unified European economy means people have more choices about where to work, companies can grow larger, and Europe becomes economically stronger. David points out that, even if Europe is one economy, it can still make sensible rules about exempting some areas, such as health care, from private company competition. It can try to protect groups of people who are thrown out of work because of fierce competition among companies. Some people in the United Kingdom say that the EU makes silly laws under the guise of creating standard and fair rules about products throughout Europe. David says the press makes up a lot of this silliness—the myth that bananas with bends in them cannot be sold, that each egg has to be stamped with information about its farm of origin, that all British and European ambulances have to be painted yellow, and that even the smallest fishing boats must carry 620 medical items.

## HOW THE EU AFFECTS DAVID

The EU does many things that are not apparent to David, but he can also see its footprints in many parts of his everyday life.

At school, David studies French as his main foreign language and German as his second. The EU encourages everyone to study two European languages outside his or her own. His school does not focus on the EU as part of an academic class, but a lot of the clubs, like the Politics Society, talk about it. David also learns about the EU in his language classes. Some of his teachers grew up in other European countries. Because the European Union allows people to travel freely across EU country borders for work, they could get teaching jobs in the

United Kingdom without going through a long process of getting a work permit.

The home stadium of the Arsenal Football Club, one of the most famous professional soccer teams in the world, is near where David lives. The older stadium at Highbury has been replaced by a shiny, new, state-of-the-art, environmentally friendly stadium nearby. Usually David watches soccer on television rather than in the stadium, and one network has been monopolizing soccer match broadcasts. The EU is breaking up this soccer broadcast monopoly. When David watches soccer or other programs, he does not see any commercials advertising cigarettes, because many years ago an EU law banned tobacco advertisements on television in all countries.

When David and his family travel to France, another EU country, for their yearly holiday, they get through immigration and customs control quickly because they hold the passport of an EU country. The EU countries have agreed that citizens of member states should be allowed to travel and work anywhere they want in the Union, and so the line for EU passport holders moves quickly, with few checks and no passport stamping. At most borders in the world, immigration officers check carefully whether people have the right to cross the border. Officers stamp travelers' passports to indicate permission to enter, and customs agents enforce rules about how much you can bring from another country without paying a special tax. But these customs checks have been abolished for members of the EU traveling between EU countries. Customs officers still check for illegal weapons and drugs, but not for legal goods people have bought abroad. Because Britain has not switched over to the currency used by many EU countries, the euro, David's family has to convert their pounds sterling into euros to buy things in France.

Most of the groceries David's parents buy originate in the United Kingdom and other EU countries, but the shops are also full of products from New Zealand, Kenya, and the Caribbean countries, which used to be colonies of the United Kingdom. In fact, the EU has given special preference to products from ex-colonies of its member states. David likes milk chocolate, especially Cadbury Milk Chocolate. There has been a long controversy in the EU about whether Cadbury Milk Chocolate can be considered real chocolate because of its ingredients. The EU had to make decisions about what could be labeled and sold as "chocolate" because of its powers to regulate trade. The EU is also strict about whether food can contain genetically modified organisms (GMOs), which are created by putting the genes of one species into another. There are few GMO foods on the shelves in the European Union because the majority of people think they are potentially dangerous and should be avoided.

On July 7, 2005, suicide bombers exploded bombs on buses and subways in London, killing 52 people, injuring many more, and destroying part of the transportation system. The day before, the people of London had been celebrating because they had won the Olympic bid for 2012. David's mother was almost on one of the trains that was bombed at 8:50 A.M. David was at school in the central business district of London when the bombs went off. He and his classmates were not permitted to leave the building for a long time, and it was hard to contact their parents because the cell phone system was shut down. Eventually, David walked home. The EU is working on ways police in different countries can work together to fight terrorism and crime.

# Europe and the European Union

THE EU IS AN ORGANIZATION OF COUNTRIES ON THE continent of Europe. It is a level of decision and lawmaking above the level of the individual country. It tries to replace rivalry between countries with a new cooperative political system. It represents countries' voluntarily giving up some powers over their own territories to cooperate with other countries in order to make decisions together. It has changed the way economies in Europe operate and relate to each other.

As the EU grows and takes on more responsibilities, it becomes important not only to political leaders but also to many people in their everyday lives. It affects people in its own member states, and people all over the world.

## THE EUROPEAN COMMUNITY

The geographic continent of Europe covers about 4 million square miles, less than 7 percent of the globe's land surface. It is bounded by seas on the north, west, and south and by the Ural Mountains and Bosporus Strait (the waterway connecting the Sea of Marmara with the Black Sea) to the east. But this definition is awkward because Russia is half in geographic Europe and half outside. A small part of Turkey lies within what geographers consider Europe, and Turkish leaders have modeled their political system on the European separation of state and religion. Most Europeans, however, consider Turkey part of Asia and Islamic civilization. The Balkan countries (Albania, Bosnia and Herzegovina, Bulgaria, Croatia, Greece, Macedonia, Romania, Serbia and Montenegro, Slovenia) also lie at the border of Europe and Asia.

Europe may be defined more by its history and way of life than by physical geography. Most of Europe shares a past shaped by ancient Greece and Rome, as well as by Judaism and Christianity. Together, these traditions emphasize the value of the individual, rational thinking and scientific inquiry, and civic responsibility. Christianity developed into Europe's major religion, often becoming an official religion supported by political power, sometimes giving rise to political intrigue, violence, and war.

Beginning in the 1400s, Europe underwent many changes. New inventions and technological changes, expanding trade, voyages of discovery to the New World, and development of industry during what is called the Industrial Revolution gradually made Europe into a major world power. In the late 1800s, European countries competed with each other to conquer and colonize less industrialized countries in Africa, Asia, and the Middle East. They worked to control territory overseas in order to increase their economic resources and political power around the globe.

European countries were often competitive and violent. They fought wars with each other and subdued peoples on

**Europe**

ICELAND
Reykjavik

ATLANTIC
OCEAN

SWEDEN    FINLAND

NORWAY    Helsinki

Oslo    Stockholm    Tallinn
                              ESTONIA

UNITED    North    RUSSIA
KINGDOM    Sea    Riga    LATVIA

DENMARK    LITHUANIA
IRELAND    Copenhagen    Vilnius    Minsk
Dublin    RUSSIA

NETHERLANDS    POLAND    BELARUS
Amsterdam
London    Berlin    Warsaw    Kiev

Brussels    GERMANY    UKRAINE
BELGIUM    CZECH
Paris    LUXEM-    REPUBLIC    SLOVAKIA    MOLDOVA
BOURG    LIECHTENSTEIN    Prague    Bratislava    Chisinau
SWITZERLAND    Vienna    Budapest    ROMANIA
FRANCE    Bern    AUSTRIA    HUNGARY    Bucharest
SLOVENIA    Black Sea
SAN    Ljubljana    Zagreb    Belgrade
MARINO    CROATIA
Sarajevo    BULGARIA
BOSNIA-    Podgorica    Sofia
ANDORRA    MONACO    ITALY    HERZEGOVINA    MONTENEGRO    MACEDONIA
PORTUGAL    Rome    Tiranë    Skopje    TURKEY
Madrid    ALBANIA
Lisbon    SPAIN    GREECE

Mediterranean Sea    Athens

Nicosia
CYPRUS
MOROCCO    ALGERIA    TUNISIA    Valletta    MALTA    © Infobase Publishing

0    400 miles
0    400 km

N

Europe is the second-smallest continent in terms of area, but the third-most populous, making up about 11 percent of the world's population. The northernmost point of the European mainland is Cape Nordkinn, in Norway; the southernmost point, Punta de Tarifa, in southern Spain, near Gibraltar. From west to east, the mainland ranges from Cabo da Roca, in Portugal, to the northeastern slopes of the Urals, in Russia.

other continents. They initiated and fought World Wars I and II. World War I created widespread destruction. About 50 million people died, including those who were killed in the flu epidemic and smaller conflicts after the war. World

War II was the largest and deadliest war in human history, resulting in 42 million deaths—two-thirds of which were civilian casualties—in Europe alone and more than 60 million deaths altogether. After World War II, avoiding war and resolving conflict through peaceful means became a guiding force in most of Europe.

Adolf Hitler's Nazi government in Germany deliberately exterminated 6 million European Jews during World War II, in what is often described as the Holocaust. At first Jewish people were not allowed to do certain everyday things, such as attend public schools or own businesses. Later, Jews were transported to death camps and used as slave labor. Other groups—disabled people, gay people, Soviet prisoners, Jehovah's Witnesses, political opponents, and Roma (sometimes called Gypsies)—were also imprisoned and killed. The Nazis and their collaborators extended their murderous campaigns to the other countries Germany invaded, and the terror finally ended in 1945 with the victory of the Allied forces. Such horrors strengthened Europe's commitment after the war to guarantee basic human rights and observe the rule of law.

European political systems today are democratic and guarantee a range of human rights. Human rights are the rights people have simply because they are human beings and need certain basic standards to live with dignity. European countries have free elections among competing political parties to fill high government offices; they grant civil liberties (freedom of speech, organization, and association) to citizens; they provide citizens with basic social protection (such as health care, sickness pay when people are too ill to work, pensions when people are too old to work); and they are guided by law. The European Union forbids the death penalty, seen as a violation of the basic human right to life, under all circumstances and works for its abolition around the world. Unions are important in the European model as a way of strengthening the voices of working people and defending their rights. Labor unions and employers are sometimes referred to as "the social partners" in European countries.

Until the 1990s, however, countries such as Poland, Romania, and Czechoslovakia in the eastern part of Europe were not democratic but run by Communist parties. These parties eliminated other, competing political parties and outlawed any organizations that criticized the ruling party. They also limited individual liberties. In general, citizens of these countries had not chosen Communist parties to rule them, but these parties won power because of certain agreements between the Soviet Union and other countries toward the end of World War II, the presence of the Soviet army, and other strategies guided by the Soviet Union.

Today, European countries have market economies, in which most economic decisions (such as what to make, how to produce things, and where to buy things) are left to individual companies. Companies tend to respond to what consumers buy. The state has owned or controlled some key industries and services, such as steel, transportation, or energy, within many of these market economies, as well as made rules and laws for the market in general. Until the collapse of Communism in the late 1980s, Eastern European countries had state-planned or state-directed economies. The state owned most of the factories and supervised agriculture. Managers working for the central state determined which goods and services would be produced at which prices. Firms did not respond to lots of different consumers but to the plan and directions of the state. Trade was strictly controlled by the government, and Communist states tended to trade only with each other and not compete with other economies.

Modern Europe as a whole is technologically advanced and wealthy compared with other regions of the world. Europeans have some of the highest standards of living and most efficient economies in the world. The average amount of resources available per person per year in Europe is equivalent to $31,960. In

Latin America and the Caribbean, on the other hand, the average is less than $4,050, while in Africa south of the Sahara desert it is less than $750.[1] Many parts of Europe, like the United States and Japan, are now "postindustrial." Most workers and resources are no longer directed to agriculture and farming or even to making goods such as machines, vehicles, clothes, and toys. These economies generally employ more people and create more value in what is called the service sector—economic activities that do not produce objects but happen mainly person to person, like teaching, or giving health care, or entertaining.

## MEMBER STATES IN THE EU

All EU member states are on the European continent, but the member states of the Union have changed over time. Six Western European states—France, Germany, Italy, the Netherlands, Belgium, and Luxembourg—were the original members of the organization. In 1973, Denmark, Ireland, and the United Kingdom joined. In 1981, Greece joined as well. And in 1986, Portugal and Spain became members. The eastern half of Germany, formerly a separate state under Com-

## MEMBERSHIP IN THE EUROPEAN COMMUNITY AND EUROPEAN UNION[2]

| 1958 | EC-6 | Belgium, Federal Republic of Germany, France, Italy, Luxembourg, Netherlands |
| 1973 | EC-9 | Denmark, Ireland, and United Kingdom join EC-6 |
| 1981 | EC-10 | Greece joins EC-9 |
| 1986 | EC-12 | Spain and Portugal join EC-10 |
| 1995 | EU-15 | Austria, Finland, and Sweden join EC-12 |
| 2004 | EU-25 | Czech Republic, Estonia, Cyprus, Latvia, Lithuania, Hungary, Malta, Poland, Slovenia, and Slovakia join EU-15 |
| 2007 | EU-27 | Bulgaria and Romania join EU-25 |

## European Union, 2008

European Union member

Applying for European Union status

0          500 miles
0      500 km

N

SWEDEN

FINLAND

ATLANTIC OCEAN

NORWAY

ESTONIA          RUSSIA

UNITED KINGDOM

*North Sea*

LATVIA

DENMARK

LITHUANIA

*Baltic Sea*

RUSSIA

IRELAND

NETHERLANDS

BELARUS

POLAND

GERMANY

UKRAINE

BELGIUM

LUXEMBOURG

CZECH REPUBLIC

SLOVAKIA

MOLDOVA

AUSTRIA

HUNGARY

ROMANIA

SWITZ.

SLOVENIA

CROATIA

*Black Sea*

FRANCE

BOSNIA AND HERCEGOVINA

SERBIA

MONTENEGRO

BULGARIA

PORTUGAL

SPAIN

ITALY

ALBANIA

MACEDONIA

TURKEY

GREECE

*Mediterranean Sea*

CYPRUS

© Infobase Publishing

MALTA

The political entity of Europe, now called the European Union, has expanded from its original six members in 1957 to 27 members in 2007. Scandinavian countries, southern European countries, and formerly Communist Eastern European countries have all joined.

munist rule, became part of a reunited Germany in 1990 and so was incorporated into the EU. In 1995, Austria, Finland, and Sweden joined. The largest and most ambitious enlargement of the European Union occurred in 2004, when eight former Communist countries plus Cyprus and Malta became part of the EU. In 2007, Bulgaria and Romania, two other former Communist countries, joined.

Including the formerly Communist countries was an impressive step toward cooperation in European politics. Between 1945 and 1989, Europe was divided by the politics of the Cold War, the tension between the United States and Soviet Union. Each superpower and its allies competed in many ways—in building up troops and dangerous weapons, in trying to control territory around the world, in developing technology and exploring space, and in ideas about politics and economics. Cold War tensions never broke into open warfare in Europe, but there were wars in Korea and Vietnam. The western European countries, such as the United Kingdom, Ireland, France, Germany, and Belgium, were democratic with market economies and aligned with the United States as a superpower. The eastern half of Europe was under the control of the Soviet Union. There was limited individual and group freedom, and the economies tended to be state-directed. When Communism fell apart in Eastern Europe around 1989, the EU played an important role in helping these countries build democratic institutions and market economies.

## HOW THE EU CHANGES POLITICS

Europe has always been divided into many countries. Today, Europe is divided into over 40, though only 27 of these are in the EU. Each country has its own constitution, government, type of economy, language or languages, and other traditions. These countries are often referred to as nation states.

In 1648, at the end of the Thirty Years' War, European powers signed the Treaty of Westphalia. It said that national states would be the main units in international politics and that no one could interfere in what was going on in other countries. The idea of the national state or nation state was that people who were similar to each other (sharing language and culture) should be able to decide what happens in their own country. They would have their own political system to make decisions that would govern their lives. They would make laws for themselves, and the state would enforce these rules in its own territory. The idea that people formed into a state should be able to make and enforce their own laws and be free from interference from outside powers is called sovereignty.

The members of the EU are nation states. But the EU changes the ability of its member states to make and enforce laws in their own territory. The EU adds a new level of government above the level of the nation state. It modifies the sovereignty of member states. Many EU decisions are binding on the national states. The EU member-states have set up new institutions to which they delegate some of their sovereignty so that decisions on specific matters of joint interest can be made at a European level.

The EU makes decisions in many, but not all, areas of politics. Formerly called the European Economic Community (EEC), the EU began by trying to break down trade barriers within Europe. Its activities now extend well beyond trade, to areas such as protecting the environment, working to improve public health, helping police cooperate across borders, and supporting economic development in poorer regions of the world. However, the EU does not make many decisions about policies such as health care and child care. It does not make laws about what should be taught in schools or define what a crime is in member states. The EU does not have a strong foreign policy and has no permanent military forces of its own.

The EU does not enforce most of the rules it makes. It expects member states to adopt EU laws as their own and then use national agencies to enforce the laws. So, for example, if the EU passes laws about what chemicals are allowed in water, it expects member states to reflect the EU rules in a national law and to use the national Department of the Environment to enforce it.

The EU has always been based on legal treaties (formal agreements between governments of nation states) and law. It has never had a basic, clear, formal constitution. A political constitution is usually a single, short, written document. It sets out a state's fundamental principles, establishes the power of different parts of the state and their relationship to each other, and grants specific rights to the people of the political unit. Its key points are relatively permanent. An EU constitution was drafted in 2004, but some member states rejected it. On December 13, 2007, EU member states signed the Treaty of Lisbon that contained some of the changes laid out in the Constitution, and the EU continues to function according to existing treaties.

## HOW THE EU CHANGES ECONOMIES

The modern state makes rules about how people can do things in the economy—what kinds of businesses are legal or illegal, who can own companies and how companies are organized, what kind of safety measures have to be followed in factories, what sorts of taxes must be paid on economic activities such as earning an income or making profits, and how goods and workers can go back and forth between countries. The economy, especially trade, is an area in which the EU has taken over a lot of decision making.

The EU has tried to encourage free trade within Europe. Modern countries trade by sending, or exporting, some of the goods or services they produce to other countries for sale. The main barriers that countries have used to try to protect their industries and peoples' livelihoods from overseas competition have been tariffs (taxes on imports or goods produced abroad entering the country), subsidies (government grants to home producers of goods), and quotas (limits on the numbers of goods that can be imported). The economic theory of free trade, or trade without these barriers, says that the larger the area over which free trade and competition take place the better it is for the economy. Countries have different natural, human, and capital resources and different ways of combining these. When regions and countries specialize in what they can produce at the lowest cost and then trade, everyone's production and consumption of goods will increase. A larger free trade area (all of Europe rather than just one or two countries) might help many companies to make and sell more. When a company produces more of one thing, the cost of each unit of the goods tends to fall. This might allow the company to make more profit or to lower its prices. A large market involves more businesses trying to produce the same thing. More competition may make companies stronger by making them compete for customers based on price and quality. Consumers benefit from lower prices. Even if a company fails or closes and people lose their jobs, advocates of free trade say this is best in the long run, because only the strongest companies remain, and businesspeople will identify other things that they can produce efficiently. The EU tries to maximize market competition both by expanding its free trade area and by limiting government involvement in the economy.

The EU goes beyond dismantling barriers to trade among its member states. The member states agree on a general EU tariff against countries outside the EU, making the EU a customs union. In the 1990s, the EU tried to make trade within Europe even easier by removing nontariff barriers, or barriers other than import taxes, and to make the Union more like a single economy or single market. These other barriers included the paperwork for products going across borders within the EU and different kinds of standards for things such as steel strength or car safety from country to country. Then the EU even introduced a common currency, or a shared money system, called

The 27 European member states retain their colorful national flags, their languages, and their institutions. The EU brings member countries together to reach common goals such as peace and security, economic prosperity, and environmental protection.

the euro. Trying to create a single market has involved the EU in policy areas such as the environment, consumer protection, and science and technology.

## SUCCESS OF THE EU

No one really expects the EU to become one united state, because Europe is composed of many peoples with their own nation states, languages, cultures, and histories. The basic idea of the European Union is unity in diversity. The question is really how well these countries have been able to cooperate to achieve their common goals.

Most commentators would say that the EU has contributed to peace and security on the European continent for more than 50 years. It has created more economic growth than might have occurred without free trade. The European Union has strengthened democracy and human rights in Europe and beyond. But there is also unhappiness about the EU in Europe. Growth rates, unemployment, and poverty are still problems in many EU countries. Many people are worried that they are losing their national traditions and values by being part of the EU. Still others say that EU decision making is not democratic, because no one votes directly for many EU decision-makers and because ordinary citizens do not really debate European issues. Fifty years after its beginnings, the EU continues to be a strong political structure, but many of the details of what it does and how it operates are controversial.

# History of the EU, 1950–1993

On May 9, 1950, in an ornate room in the French Ministry for Foreign Affairs, Robert Schuman, France's foreign minister, made the "Schuman Declaration." He spoke in a hesitant and monotonous voice to the gathered heads of government and about 200 newspaper reporters, but people soon realized the importance of his announcement. He proposed that France, Germany, and other democratic countries should establish a "community" to regulate together their coal and steel industries. Schuman was a religious, peace-oriented Catholic who came from a steelmaking area that Germany and France had fought over for decades. May 9, the date of his speech, continues to be celebrated as "Europe Day" throughout Europe.

Even though Schuman made the announcement, it was Jean Monnet, another Frenchman, who had drawn up the plan.

Foreign ministers of six participating European countries signed the Paris Treaty creating the European Coal and Steel Community on April 18, 1951. French foreign minister Robert Schuman (*seated*) proposed in 1950 that several countries, including France and Germany, allow their coal and steel industries to be regulated by a European "community."

For many decades, Monnet had been thinking about how to prevent war in Europe and get European countries to cooperate more. The German head of government in 1950, Konrad Adenauer, supported the Schuman proposal. Also a Catholic, he had been mayor of a big city in Germany before Adolf Hitler, the dictatorial Nazi leader of Germany from 1934 to 1945, sent him to prison with other political opponents.

The Schuman Declaration was the birth of European integration, or the combining of the separate European nation states into a new entity of Europe. It made sense that political leaders focused on the iron and steel sector at first. World War II remained fresh in people's minds, and iron and steel had been used to build weapons. Sharing iron and steel industries would be a good way of discouraging war. Coal, iron, and steel are also essential to peacetime economies as steel is used in constructing buildings, making transportation networks and vehicles, and building big machines and tools used in factories. Europe needed to recover from wartime devastation. As the Cold War unfolded, European and U.S. leaders thought that strengthening Europe's economies would prevent the extension of Soviet influence into Western Europe.

The "original six"—Germany, France, Luxembourg, Netherlands, Belgium, and Italy—signed the European Coal

## JEAN MONNET

Jean Monnet (1888–1979) was a founding father of European integration. He was born in the small town of Cognac in France. Monnet was eager to enter "the school of life," so he never finished high school. At 16, he entered the family cognac (an alcoholic drink) business and became an apprentice in London. At the outbreak of World War I, he helped acquire and coordinate military supplies for Britain and France, and he played a similar role during World War II. He was friendly with U.S. president Franklin D. Roosevelt during the war, and he admired the American Constitution.

After World War II, Monnet was a leader in reconstructing and modernizing the French economy, bringing together business leaders, political parties, and labor unions. He assumed a central role in developing proposals for European integration. He and Steel Community Treaty in 1951. The ECSC officially came into existence in July 1952. The ECSC tried to ensure that governments and companies that needed coal and steel would be able to get quality materials, quickly, at good prices. They thought that fair competition without unfair subsidies or tariff barriers between countries would contribute to this goal. Another aim of the ECSC was for workers in coal and steel to have improved working conditions, fair wages, and the ability to work in these industries in any country.

## THE TREATY OF ROME

In 1957, in Rome, representatives of the same six countries that signed the ECSC treaty signed a new treaty, the Treaty of Rome.

designed the European Coal and Steel Community (ECSC) and helped lay the foundation for the Treaty of Rome (1957), which set up the European Economic Community.

Monnet saw European integration as a moral as well as a political project, one that could prevent war, create social and economic security, and support economic prosperity. Problems of coordination during wartime, as well as the failures of the League of Nations (where he was deputy general-secretary between the World Wars), taught Monnet that national sovereignty could make leaders think too narrowly and prevent strong cooperation. In his long quest to build a more cooperative Europe, Monnet emphasized creating new institutions that helped people think in terms of more general interests and work on their problems together.

Giant paintings showing a legendary conflict between the leaders of two ancient cities, Rome and Alba, decorated the walls. The building in which the signing took place was located in the middle of a public square designed by the Renaissance artist and architect Michelangelo. It was an appropriate location for the signing of a treaty meant to put an end to war in Europe and bring together European nation states.

Many countries and leaders were involved with this proposal, but Germany and France were still the main partners. Because they had been the main adversaries in the two World Wars, their partnership continued to be important. They had large economies. The French wanted to sell their own agricultural products (livestock, grain, fruits, and vegetables) and those of their colonies and former colonies (wine, citrus fruit, sugarcane, bananas) throughout Europe. But their agriculture was relatively high cost and not very efficient, so some subsidies would help. They also wanted free trade in industrial products. The Germans wanted freer trade in the industrial products that they made—machinery, chemicals, and electrical goods—but also saw advantages to a common market and strong agriculture, since they were short of food. The other countries in Europe wanted Germany inside the European Economic Community as a way of controlling the country that had so recently initiated such a destructive worldwide war.

The 1957 Treaty of Rome built upon the ECSC but took some big steps forward. It created the European Economic Community (EEC). The preamble to the Rome Treaty promised "foundations of an ever-closer union among the peoples of Europe." Article 2 said,

> The Community shall have as its task . . . to promote throughout the Community a harmonious and balanced development of economic activities, a continuous and balanced expansion, an increase in stability, an

European leaders gathered in Rome in 1957 to sign a new treaty that would extend the original European Coal and Steel Community to include development of a common market across industries and services. The Treaty of Rome created the European Economic Community (EEC).

accelerated rise in living standards, and closer relations between the States belonging to it.[3]

The new Treaty of Rome extended economic coordination from joint control of iron and steel alone to broader economic cooperation and free trade across all sectors and goods. Taking effect in 1958, it created a "common market." The treaty provided for the elimination of all tariffs, or taxes on imports, among members of the union. The member states also wanted to encourage movement of workers, companies, and goods and services across borders so that the economies of the separate member states would become more like one large economy or a single market. The treaty made the EEC a "customs union" that combined free trade inside with a common tariff on goods coming from outside the member states. The member states

 **CHOCOLATE**

When Britain joined the European Union in 1973, existing EU member states and the European Union defined "chocolate" as dark chocolate, made with a high percentage of cocoa and cocoa butter, not with dairy products or with other vegetable fat. Britain specialized in making milk chocolate and often added other vegetable fats. It got special permission to call its recipe "chocolate," but other countries did not want to import it. The British argued that these countries were creating a nontariff barrier to free trade. Developing countries in Africa, especially the Ivory Coast, exported cocoa butter to European chocolate makers and wanted to keep cocoa butter as the only fat.

In 1999, the European Union made a compromise. Milk chocolate bars of about 20 percent milk and with up to 5 percent vegetable fat would be cleared for sale on the continent if labeled Family Milk Chocolate and/or labeled with a statement about the vegetable fats. Even once this law was passed, Spain and Italy refused to allow British chocolate—which they said could not be compared to Belgian, French, Spanish, and Italian chocolate—to enter their markets. In 2003, the European Court of Justice ordered Spain and Italy to lift a ban on the sale of British chocolate. The court said, "The characteristic element of all products bearing the name chocolate is the presence of a certain minimum cocoa and cocoa butter content. The addition

agreed to establish a common agricultural policy that commit-
ted a large part of the EEC's budget to keeping the prices of
agricultural goods high. Farmers could then use the income
to invest in their farms, produce more food, and enjoy good
living standards. It was also agreed that the EEC would create
a special fund to help poorer regions in the EEC.

**Supermarkets in London stock Cadbury Dairy Milk Chocolate and
other British specialties, which were at the center of EU chocolate
controversies.**

of vegetable fats does not substantially alter the nature of those
products."* The British Department of Trade was pleased, saying
that finally, after 30 years, there would be a true single market in
chocolate, and consumers all over Europe could decide to buy
Terry's chocolate oranges, Cadbury's Dairy Milk chocolate bars,
and other British favorites.

* Andrew Osborn, "Chocolate War Over After 30 Years," Guardian, January 17,
2003. Available online at *http://www.guardian.co.uk/uk/2003/jan/17/foodanddrink.*

The treaty was very general, setting out objectives and timetables for moving forward in these areas. Over the next several decades, it would be the job of the European institutions to draw up plans of action and pass legislation to achieve the treaty objectives. The customs union occurred in July 1968, 18 months ahead of schedule, with the lifting of customs inspections and charges at borders and the imposition of a common external tariff for imports from nonmembers. Other work on the freedoms of movement was complicated and slow.

The EEC's decision-making institutions were modeled on those of the ECSC. A European Commission would propose policies and laws that helped realize the treaty's general objectives. It would try to represent and strengthen the community as a whole. A Council of Ministers, ministers from each member state, would vote for or against the commission's proposals. A European Parliament would consult with the commission. A European Court of Justice would ensure that the treaty was being followed and that national governments were following EU law.

## NEW MEMBERS OF THE EEC, 1970s–1990s

In the 1970s, other countries joined the European Economic Community (EEC). In January 1973, the United Kingdom joined. Originally the United Kingdom was not interested in the ECSC or the EEC. It wanted to keep strong ties to its former colonies, now organized in what was called the British Commonwealth, and to the United States. It thought of itself as a world power, not just a European one. But over time, Britain saw that its ties to the Commonwealth and its global power were weakening, and the economies of the EEC countries were doing better than the United Kingdom's. However, the EEC rejected Britain's first two applications to join. General Charles DeGaulle, then the president of France, instigated the rejections. He thought that the United Kingdom might challenge France's strong role in the EEC, and worried that the

United Kingdom might try to slow down integration or allow the United States more influence. Britain only was able to join after DeGaulle resigned from the French presidency in 1969. Denmark and Ireland also joined in 1973.

In the 1980s, three Mediterranean countries—Greece, Spain, and Portugal—joined the EEC. When European integration first began, these countries were not democracies, and the original six countries did not want to associate closely with them. But as these countries emerged in the middle 1970s from decades of dictatorship, the EEC countries became more interested. Greece, Spain, and Portugal were also poorer countries, with large agricultural sectors. They wanted to join both to be part of the economic common market and to be seen as part of democratic Europe. In the early 1990s, a few more countries—Austria, Finland, and Sweden—joined the European Union. In the 1960s and 1970s, Austria and Sweden did not want to join because they wanted to be neutral during the Cold War, and the EEC was clearly identified as in the U.S. sphere. They were also members of another free trade area. But as the rivalry between the United States and Soviet Union weakened, and as the EEC proved strong, their interest grew. These democratic, prosperous countries already incorporated many of the community's standards into their national laws.

## THE SINGLE MARKET PROJECT, 1980s AND 1990s

On the twenty-fifth anniversary of the Treaty of Rome, in the early 1980s, many political leaders thought that the promises of the treaty had not been realized. Businesspeople said that, even though tariff barriers had been removed, nontariff barriers remained. European economies were lagging behind the United States and Japan in competitiveness. A British magazine put a tombstone on its cover to say that the EEC was as good as dead.

To revive European integration, Frenchman Jacques Delors led a project to dismantle nontariff barriers and create a single market. At the time he did this, he was president of the European Commission, one of the main decision-making bodies in the EU. Many changes were written into a new treaty, called the Single European Act (SEA), which came into effect in 1987. The main aims of the SEA were to create a larger market and replace national regulation with new Europe-wide regulations. Physical barriers, like different kinds of paperwork for goods going between countries, made trade difficult. Technical barriers, like different regulations about drug safety, different requirements about how strong steel had to be to be used in buildings or cars, or different requirements to be an electrician or dentist in different countries, stood in the way. Different kinds of taxes in different countries made it hard for companies to do business in different places.

The EEC began to develop a policy to regulate environmental pollution and quality. Environmental policy seemed essential to fair trade. Companies that face weaker environmental laws usually have lower costs; they do not have to spend money controlling what goes into the air through smokestacks or vents, for example. They can gain an unfair competitive edge and sell more cheaply. Also, unclean air and water go across boundaries and so are problems ideally regulated at the European level. The EEC also faced demands from workers and some businesses to regulate working conditions across countries so that businesses in all countries had to follow certain health and safety rules, such as limits on the amount of weight someone could lift at work or how long someone could work without a break. If the EEC was giving business more freedom to trade and compete, the commission and ministers realized they also needed to give workers more protection. The EEC strengthened its funds for less-developed regions in Europe, understanding that a more open market might exaggerate poverty in some regions and wealth in others, and divide parts of Europe from each other.

EEC leaders also figured out how to make it easier to pass all these regulations. For most of these economic measures, instead of all countries in the Council of Ministers having to agree, it became possible to pass laws with a majority of votes. At the same time, the European Parliament got more powers. The Parliament, since 1979 directly elected by citizens of member states, was the EEC institution closest to the people. As Europe's powers expanded and people increasingly felt the impact of decisions in their everyday lives, it was important to strengthen the power of the representatives of the people in the EEC Parliament. At first, the European Commission recommended about 300 new measures to make the single market, but by 2002, there were 1,475 new rules.[4] Some nontariff barriers remained, especially in services, transportation, and government buying of goods and services.

# History of the EU, 1990–Today

MANY POLITICAL LEADERS WANTED TO TAKE THE EUROPEAN Economic Community further. In the Treaty on European Union, signed at Maastricht in the Netherlands in 1991 and amended by the treaties of Amsterdam and Nice, the union became closer, more powerful, and better organized. The European Economic Community became the EU.

## THE MAASTRICHT TREATY

The Maastricht Treaty established "citizenship of the European Union." Citizens of the EU acquired many rights. They have the right of residence and the right to move freely anywhere in the Union; the right to vote and run as candidates in local elections in any member state in which they are living, even if it is not their home country; the right to vote and run in elections in the

European Parliament in their state of residence; and the right to petition the European Parliament. Being an EU citizen is the right of every person who is a citizen of an individual member state. EU citizenship does not replace but exists alongside national state citizenship.

European institutions gained powers from the treaty in such areas as public health, consumer protection, education, training and culture, energy policy, and foreign policy. Maastricht strengthened the role of the European Parliament and changed other aspects of decision making.

The Maastricht Treaty also set the stage for a single currency and new rule-making about the economy. With a common currency, countries have the same money with the same value, and this money can move freely across borders. With different national currencies, one currency must be converted to another, and the exchange rate (for example, how many French francs are equivalent to one Deutsche mark) would vary from day to day. In order to join the euro currency and to stay inside the common currency, national governments had to follow certain rules about their spending. A European Central Bank was put in charge of the currency. In 2002, most member states introduced a shared European currency, the euro. For some nation states, including the United Kingdom, Denmark, and Sweden, this was going too far in giving up national control over their economy, and they stayed outside the Eurozone, keeping their own national currencies.

Through the Maastricht Treaty, Europe got more powers in areas of foreign and security policy and in police and criminal matters. For example, Europe was a lead negotiator with Iran over its nuclear program and has played an important role in the ongoing Israeli-Palestinian peace process. Within Europe, there is now cooperation in fighting terrorism and crime, including a common European arrest warrant that makes it easier to send suspected criminals across borders for arrest and trials. In these two new areas, decisions still are made by the agreement of all countries, with the possibility of one country voting no and defeating the proposal.

## ENLARGEMENT

By the late 1980s, Communism was falling apart in the Soviet Union. Many of the countries in Eastern and Central Europe that had been part of the Soviet Union's sphere of influence were adopting private ownership and market economies and forms of democracy. Most of these countries had a difficult time making the transition from Communism to market democracies. Economically, the first 10 years after the fall of Communism were even worse than the Great Depression of the 1930s in the United States; the total amount of goods and services produced fell, people became poorer, and unemployment was high. Almost all of these countries wanted to join the EU, both to improve their economies and to become part of democratic Europe.

The EU wanted to assist the Central and Eastern European countries—Poland, Hungary, the Czech Republic, Slovakia, Slovenia, Estonia, Latvia, and Lithuania. But the existing member states were not sure if they actually wanted these countries to join the EU. Germany was an active supporter, while France worried about threats to their markets from cheap industrial goods and agricultural products. Spain was concerned it would lose a lot of the financial assistance it was getting as a poorer member. Working people worried that many workers from these countries would migrate to Western Europe for jobs, once they had freedom of movement, or that companies would move to these lower-cost economies and leave Western Europeans without jobs. There were concerns about how much it would cost to support these countries' agriculture in line with the common agricultural policy established in the Treaty of Rome. But admitting these countries would strengthen democracy, stability, and

Here, an elderly man and his grandson search through Dumpsters in a small village in Poland. Countries in the former Soviet bloc fell on hard times after the fall of Communism. Production decreased dramatically, while poverty and unemployment affected almost everyone. The EU worked with these countries to build new economies and political systems, and eventually admitted them to the EU.

peace in the region. Economic opportunities both for existing and new member states would increase. Many people thought that it was morally right to welcome these countries, recently liberated from Soviet control, back to the Europe in which they belonged.

In June 1993, the heads of governments in the EU said they would like to admit these new countries, once the countries met certain conditions for membership. The conditions, called the Copenhagen criteria, were:

> Membership requires that the candidate country has
> achieved stability of institutions guaranteeing democracy,
> the rule of law, human rights and respect for minorities,
> the existence of a functioning market economy as well
> as the capacity to cope with competitive pressure and
> market forces within the Union. Membership presup-
> poses the candidate's ability to take on the obligations of
> membership including adherence to the aims of politi-
> cal, economic and monetary union.[5]

The more detailed requirements for membership included
acceptance and adoption of what is called the acquis com-
munautaire. These are all the principles, policies, laws, and
practices that have been agreed to in the EU from its origin.
They include all the main treaties, legislation, judgments by the
European Court of Justice, and other joint actions taken in the
foreign policy and criminal affairs areas. New members must
recognize that European law is primary in those areas that it
exists. The acquis are now about 80,000 pages long, divided
into more than 30 chapters, and much longer than they were
for the first new applicants to join the EEC.

In May 2004, the Eastern and Central European countries
were finally admitted, along with Malta and Cyprus. The EU
had become a regional organization of 25 member states, with
20 official languages. Europe had become the world's largest
economy and trading block, with a population of about 455
million people, extending its borders toward the boundaries
of the geographic continent.

Because the Irish prime minister, Bertie Ahern, was president of the European Council, there was a special ceremony
in Dublin, the capital of Ireland. Ahern welcomed the new
members and said it was a day of "hope and opportunity" and
that Europe had moved from "war to peace."[6] Young people
from all 25 countries presented their national flags, which were
raised together alongside the EU flag, which has a dark blue

Leaders of several EU countries watch as the Prime Minister of Cyprus, Tassos Papadopoulos, accepts his country's flag during an EU enlargement ceremony. The 2004 ceremony marked the entry of 10 new members, mainly Central and Eastern European countries, into the EU.

background and a circle of 12 gold stars representing harmony and solidarity of the member states. A mass choir sang Beethoven's "Ode to Joy," the EU national anthem. Not everyone was celebrating, though. Hundreds of protesters from different groups were there, protesting against a Europe that put free trade and business profits before the well-being of people.

Expansion is still on the agenda, but no one is sure just how far east the enlargements can go. Romania and Bulgaria joined in 2007. Talks on accession started with Turkey on October 3, 2005. Many of the Balkan countries—Bosnia, Croatia, Albania, Macedonia, and Serbia—are interested in joining. So, too, are former Soviet Republics, such as Ukraine and Belarus.

## A NEW CONSTITUTION FOR EUROPE

From its founding, the EU was based on laws, and there were constitutional elements in all its treaties—the European Coal and Steel Community Treaty, the Treaty of Rome, the Single European Act, the Treaty on European Union (Maastricht), and the Amsterdam and Nice treaties. But the provisions of these treaties, combined over time, were not clear to EU citizens, or in some cases to political leaders themselves. In view

 **THE QUESTION OF TURKEY**

Turkey has been trying to enter the EU since 1963. In 1987, Turkey formally applied for EU membership. It was officially recognized as a candidate in 1999. On October 3, 2005, Turkey and the EU began negotiations.

Turkey would be the first majority Muslim country in the EU. One argument for admitting Turkey is that it will strengthen relations between Europe and Islamic countries and show that a democratic Muslim country is possible. But one argument people make against Turkish membership is that it does not fit into Europe's predominantly Westernized and Christian culture.

Turkey is also poorer than most other EU countries. Turkey's average per capita income is about the same as that of Bulgaria and Romania and not much lower than that of Latvia. The two main cities, Istanbul and Ankara, are quite wealthy, but in the poorest areas of Turkey, near the Iranian border, people still live in mud-roofed houses and draw water from village wells. Some Europeans worry that, because of poverty or unemployment, many Turks will move to Western Europe, taking away jobs from residents and bringing a rural Turkish culture. But there are already many Turks of the deepening and widening of Europe since its founding, a new constitution would allow updating and redesigning of the political institutions. A constitutional convention completed a draft constitution in 2003.

The member states signed the EU Constitution in 2004. The mayor of Rome celebrated the historic occasion, with 25 national flags and one European flag flying in the public square. He hoped that the European dream of peace, brotherly

living in some European countries, and membership is not likely to add many more. Also, given Europe's falling birthrate and aging population, an influx of younger Turks might help. If being a member of the EU helps the Turkish economy, fewer Turks might migrate. In Turkey, as in many other countries, more regional and global trade might create economic benefits for some people, especially those who are better educated, live in cities, or work for larger companies, while making everyday life harder for others.

Turkey has already done a lot to meet the Copenhagen criteria, but there is more to do. It has abolished the death penalty, revised the criminal code, prohibited torture, and improved the rights of women. But while Turkey has adopted these new laws, it does not seem as though they are being followed everywhere in the country. The biggest ethnic minority in Turkey is the Kurds, who number about 15 million. They have fought a guerilla war with Turkey to try to get more power to rule themselves or even to have a completely separate country. Respecting the human rights of the Kurds continues to be an issue as Turkey works to join the EU.

coexistence, and understanding between individuals, peoples, and religions would be realized. He particularly emphasized the importance of young people to the future of Europe.[7]

The next step was for each member state to approve the document, either by elected parliamentary representatives or in a referendum, which is a direct vote by citizens. In May and June 2004, citizens in two countries, the Netherlands and France, voted no, after 10 other countries (Germany, Slovakia, Greece, Italy, Lithuania, Slovenia, Spain, Hungary, Austria, and Bulgaria) accepted the constitution.

Why did the Dutch and French people vote against the constitution? Many felt that the EU was expanding too far and too fast. Turkey, a predominantly Muslim and poorer country, was next on the list for possible accession. To others, like the Dublin protesters, the EU had focused too much on business profits and free markets, endangering jobs and communities. In France, many people felt that there was too much emphasis on free trade and competition and too little on protecting the livelihoods of workers and their families. Some may have voted against the EU Constitution because they were angry with their own national political leaders and national economies. Others did not like some of the provisions in the new constitution. In general, the leaders of the EU acknowledged they had a problem to solve; the leaders were out of touch with the citizens of the EU, and they had to figure out how to make the European Union better understood and more actively embraced by EU citizens. While not addressing all these concerns, the Lisbon Treaty, signed in December 2007 made some key changes in how the EU functions.

# How the
# EU Decides

THE EU IS STILL EVOLVING IN TERMS OF ITS MEMBERS
and its powers, but it has always been an organization based
upon treaties among governments. The treaties have elements of a constitution in them. They set out main objectives of the political system of the EU, define specific EU
institutions and their powers, explain the relationship of
different institutions to each other, and specify the rights of
EU citizens.

According to the treaties, the EU does not take the place of
nation-state governments and decision makers. Some powers
remain at the national level. Where a treaty has assigned authority to the Union, EU law takes precedence over national law.
In general, the view in the treaties is that nation states should
solve their own problems whenever they are able to do so.

The EU institutions are there to help nation states solve problems that require cooperation.

There are three ways in which nation states and the EU share authority. Over some areas, the EU has exclusive, or sole, authority (also referred to as competency). This is the case in issues of regulating trade within the EU, tariffs between the EU as a whole and outside countries, and the euro. Regarding the environment and energy policy, the EU and member states share authority. In areas such as penalties for specific crimes, whether the government builds low-cost housing, or who is qualified to teach and what courses are taught in schools, authority is reserved to the nation states.

The EU makes different kinds of decisions. Some are binding laws. One kind of law is called a directive. A directive specifies a goal and ways of achieving it, but the member state has to implement, or carry out, the direc-

## THE MAIN TREATIES

| DATE INTO EFFECT | NAME |
| --- | --- |
| 1958 (signed 1957) | The Treaty of Rome |
| 1987 (1986) | The Single European Act |
| 1993 (1992) | The Treaty on European Union (Maastricht) |
| 1999 (1997) | The Treaty of Amsterdam |
| 2003 (2001) | The Treaty of Nice |

There have also been accession treaties, or new treaties whenever new countries have joined, and two budget treaties. The new Constitutional Treaty would join together, simplify, and replace all of these treaties, but each country has not yet approved it.

tive through its own legal and policy system. Regulations take effect directly and immediately and generally do not require the member state to do anything. Other decisions are recommendations.

## MAKING DECISIONS WITHIN THE EU

If an area is within EU authority, there is still a question of which decision-making bodies make the decisions and how they decide. The decision-making bodies are usually referred to as the EU institutions. The three key institutions are the European Commission, the Council of Ministers, and the European Parliament. Conflicts in the EU are not only between nation states but also between institutions. The institutions check, limit, and balance each other.

The main decision-making institutions, the European Commission, the Council of Ministers, and the European Parliament, together with the European Court of Justice, are located in different parts of Europe. The main cities in which these institutions are located are sometimes referred to as the European capital cities. One Swiss writer has said that the European capitals, in the middle of historical battlefields of World Wars I and II, are located like stitches in a wound that must never reopen.[8]

Brussels, the capital of Belgium, is usually thought of as the capital of the EU because the commission, the Council of Ministers, and sometimes the European Parliament meet here. EU buildings occupy a whole area of downtown Brussels, named the Schuman district after EU founder Robert Schuman. Most of the full meetings of the European Parliament take place in Strasbourg. Strasbourg is an ancient cathedral city in Alsace, a part of France that borders Germany; Germany and France have frequently fought to control Alsace.

## The European Commission

The European Commission takes an overview of the process of European integration. At times it has acted like an engine powering the process of European integration, moving the EU forward. The commissioners who head the organization swear when they take office "to be completely independent in the performance of [their] duties [and to] neither seek nor take instructions from any other body."[9] They do not take directions from the government of the member state in which they are citizens. Instead, they try to decide, based on their best thinking and discussion with each other, what is good for the EU as a whole.

According to the treaties, only the European Commission can propose laws. Often it does not act on its own ideas but translates the aims of other groups into concrete proposals. It ensures that the treaties and laws are observed and carried out. It represents the EU internationally, particularly on trade issues.

The president of the commission, who leads planning and meetings, is agreed on by the member-state governments. Commissioners are nominated by member-state governments. The president assigns each of the 27 top-level Commissioners responsibility for a certain area of work. Each area of work is called a "service," or a Directorate General (DG). Some examples of DGs are Competition, Agriculture and Fisheries, Internal Market, and Employment and Social Affairs. There is a separate DG that oversees enlargement, which is the inclusion of new member states in the EU. Each service has many experts.

## The Council of Ministers (The Council of the European Union)

According to the Treaty of Rome, the Council of Ministers decided on its own whether to pass laws proposed by the European Commission, but now it often "co-legislates," or passes laws jointly, with the European Parliament. In this sense, the

The EU headquarters is located in Brussels, Belgium, in an area named after Robert Schuman, who first proposed the idea of a unified, European community. One of the newest buildings in the district, the Berlaymont building features heat sensors to help promote efficient use of energy and bulletproof glass and special walls to protect its staff.

EU legislature is now bicameral, or has two bodies, similar to the U.S. Congress. The Council of Ministers is composed of top cabinet officials from the governments of the member states, but it acts like a representative assembly, such as the U.S. Congress or British parliament, in passing laws.

The ministers are representatives of their nation-state governments, and they continue to hold high office in their member states while also meeting in the council. Their staffs—thousands of experts—are also recruited from and represent the nation states. The council itself, unlike the commission, is not just one, stable group of people. There are different Councils of Ministers, depending upon which issues are being discussed. Health ministers discuss health questions, environment ministers discuss EU environment policy, and economy ministers discuss economic issues.

In the council, member states vote in proportion to population. Currently, the number of votes in the council for each country is as follows: Germany, France, Italy, and the United Kingdom: 29; Spain and Poland: 27; Romania and the Netherlands: 14; Belgium, Czech Republic, Greece, Hungary, and Portugal: 12; Austria, Bulgaria, and Sweden: 10; Denmark, Ireland, Lithuania, Slovakia, and Finland: 7; Cyprus, Estonia, Latvia, Luxembourg, and Slovenia: 4; Malta: 3. On most issues, the council makes a decision based upon qualified majority voting, or 255 votes out of a total of 345. On sensitive issues such as foreign policy, the whole council must unanimously agree to a decision.

## The European Parliament

Citizens of the EU vote for members of the European Parliament (MEPs) every five years. At the founding of the European Union, member-state governments appointed the Parliament, but since 1979, citizens of the member states have directly elected representatives. The current Parliament has 785 members, about one-third of whom are women. The number of representatives elected from each country is dependent upon population. Germany has the largest delegation with 99 members; France, Italy, and the United Kingdom have 72. The smallest delegations are from Malta (5), Estonia, Cyprus, and Luxembourg (6).

Since the Maastricht Treaty, Parliament passes laws jointly with the council in many areas, such as the EU market, health, and consumer protection. The European Parliament passes laws based on majority vote, like legislatures in national political

Presidents and prime ministers of all member countries gather several times a year at the European Council to make important decisions on policy and budget issues, while also reviewing the progress on previously made decisions.

systems. Parliament must agree to international agreements negotiated by the commission and any proposed enlargement of the EU. Parliament also supervises the commission; it receives regular reports, approves or rejects nominations to the commission, and may criticize or even dismiss the commission as a whole. It must approve the EU budget.

Parliamentarians represent the citizens of member states, but they also think of themselves as part of a European Parliament and work and sit in Europe-wide political groupings. The two main political groupings are the European People's Party and European Democrats group and the European Socialists group. These and five other groupings represent different ideas about how much power Europe should have and in what ways the EU and member states should regulate private corporations and market competition.

## Other Institutions

The European Council (not to be confused with the Council of the European Union) is the meeting of heads of state or government of the member states and the commission president. The European Council meets twice a year to set general direction for the EU institutions; to make other big decisions on issues such as the economy, enlargement, or energy policy; and to settle any big arguments about the EU budget.

The European Court of Justice (ECJ) provides the legal framework for the EU. It ensures that EU treaty and other laws are applied fairly and uniformly across all member states and that member states and EU institutions do what the law requires. It also resolves disputes between EU institutions, member states, businesses, and individuals. Cases can get to the court in several ways. The ECJ has handed down thousands of decisions, speeding the development of the internal market. It has also created other kinds of standards, such as antidiscrimination standards, for the EU. It includes one senior judge per member state.

## THE THREE PILLARS

Which institutions make the decisions depends upon what kinds of decisions are being made, whether they are about the market, foreign affairs, or policing and criminal law. The EU's work can be thought of as having three pillars. Pillar One focuses on the common market. A law in this pillar is passed after the commission proposes it and the Council of Ministers agrees by a qualified majority vote (about 255 out of 345). In addition, the Parliament must approve the law. Pillar Two is the Common Security and Foreign Policy. In Pillar Two, the council must pass the law unanimously. It cooperates with the European Council (the heads of state), the commission, and the Parliament. Pillar Three is called Justice and Home Affairs or Police and Judicial Cooperation. In these areas, decisions are often made between governments and by unanimous Council of Minister decisions. The European Parliament does not have a role. Pillar One makes the EU look like a unified political system that goes beyond the member states. The triangle of institutions—the commission, council, and Parliament—is all-important in Pillar One.

# The European
# Economy

THE EU HAS THE LARGEST ECONOMY IN THE WORLD, with a 2006 gross domestic product (GDP), or total value of goods and services produced, of more than $13 trillion. The second-largest economy, the U.S. economy, has a GDP nearly as large. Within the EU, the size of member state economies varies, with many new Eastern European member states having lower total GDPs. The new Eastern European countries, which are poorer, are growing more quickly, while some of the wealthier countries are growing more slowly. Economists use the GDP divided by the population to give a better idea of overall wealth and standard of living. The higher the GDP per person (per capita), the wealthier a country is. By these measures, Europe as a whole is wealthy, but there is a lot of variation among countries.

## THE EU ECONOMIES 2006

| COUNTRY | GDP (PPP)(BILLION$) | GDP GROWTH RATE | GDP/CAPITA ($) |
|---|---|---|---|
| EU-25 | 12, 954 | 2.8 | |
| Austria | 287 | 2.8 | 34,803 |
| Belgium | 338 | 2.7 | 32,450 |
| Cyprus | 19 | 3.5 | 22,276 |
| Denmark | 196 | 2.7 | 36,074 |
| Finland | 172 | 3.5 | 32,822 |
| France | 1,900 | 2.4 | 30,150 |
| Germany | 2,605 | 2.0 | 31,571 |
| Greece | 261 | 3.7 | 23,519 |
| Ireland | 180 | 5.8 | 42,859 |
| Italy | 1,727 | 1.5 | 29,406 |
| Luxembourg | 33 | 4.0 | 72,855 |
| Netherlands | 524 | 2.9 | 32,062 |
| Portugal | 210 | 1.2 | 19,949 |
| Spain | 1,145 | 3.4 | 27,542 |
| Sweden | 283 | 4.0 | 31,264 |
| United Kingdom | 1,912 | 2.7 | 31,585 |
| Czech Republic | 199 | 6.0 | 19,428 |
| Estonia | 24 | 9.5 | 17,802 |
| Hungary | 180 | 4.5 | 17,821 |
| Latvia | 32 | 11.0 | 13,875 |
| Lithuania | 53 | 6.8 | 15,443 |
| Malta | 8 | 1.6 | 20,365 |
| Poland | 526 | 5.0 | 13,797 |
| Slovakia | 93 | 6.5 | 17,239 |
| Slovenia | 46 | 4.2 | 23,159 |
| Romania | 204 | 5.5 | 9,446 |
| Bulgaria | 77 | 5.6 | 10,003 |
| United States | 12,939 | 3.4 | 43,236 |

Source: International Monetary Fund, World Economic Outlook Database, September 2006.[10]

The EU accounts for one-fifth of all exports and imports in the world. It is the world's biggest importer and second-biggest exporter of agricultural products.[11] It represents all its member states and speaks with one voice in the World Trade Organization, which writes the rules for global trade.

Europe has gone a long way toward creating a single market, or a unified economy, such as we find in a single country. The EU was quickly able to remove tariffs on both industrial and agricultural goods among its member states. However, it continues to work to remove other, nontariff barriers to free movement of services, goods, labor, and wealth.

## FREE MOVEMENT OF SERVICES

The debate about a new law to establish a single market in services in 2005 and 2006 showed many of the interesting dilemmas of the EU in trying to push forward the single market. Services—economic activity that involves activities and skills but does not produce manufactured goods—are now two-thirds of all activities and jobs in the EU.

In 2005 and 2006, the European Commission proposed measures to create more freedom of movement in many types of services. The draft directive said that businesses would only have to follow the rules of the country in which they were based, not the rules of the country (other than their own) in which they were doing business. Because of the huge opposition to the proposal, the European Parliament and others agreed on a compromise measure. The compromise makes it easier for service companies to work across borders, but it requires that companies have to respect the legal standards of the country in which they are operating.

Small companies in many countries were in favor of the original proposal. For example, the owner of a small British advertising company would have just needed to follow the rules of the British Advertising Standards authority, even if she was doing advertising for a company based in Poland or Sweden. This would help her business because she could not afford to hire lawyers to study every country's rules about advertising or afford to make a mistake and then face a big lawsuit. Unlike in the United Kingdom, in Germany businesses cannot offer lifetime guarantees on products, and in France, they cannot offer discounts above a certain amount.[12]

Polish leaders said the new law with the country of origin idea was good for them. As a lower-cost country with lots of small- and medium-size businesses, a small market, and high unemployment, Poland's economic leaders would have liked it to be as easy as possible to provide services in other EU countries.

Unions from all over Europe, on the other hand, staged a huge demonstration on Valentine's Day 2006 to tell the European Parliament not to "break their hearts" by passing the original services directive. Amicus, Britain's largest private sector union with more than one million members, argued that employers could bring in workers at lower wage levels and with lower expectations about workplace safety. Employers could bypass an agreement with the union about pay and working conditions or could get around British laws that were better than the EU minimum by using workers from a lower-wage economy. Then employers would try to lower the wages of their U.K. workers.[13] Unions that organized workers in public services argued that the quality of health care, education, and cultural work could suffer.

## FREE MOVEMENT OF GOODS

The free movement of services seemed more difficult to resolve than free movement of manufactured products. After the Single European Act passed in 1987, the EU made progress in creating a single set of regulations for goods. More than 80 percent of standards are now the product of European or international standardization bodies instead of national standards, compared with 20 percent 15 years ago.[14] EU-level standard setting and regulation have helped goods be bought and sold all over the EU. For car making, for example, the European Union made one set of regulations about the strength of steel, the performance of engines, and the reliability of brakes in cars.

## FREE MOVEMENT OF LABOR

People do not move as easily as goods in the EU. People create lives around family and friends, they speak certain languages, and they are educated and trained within a national education system that may not easily transfer. In fact, the people who move for work in the single market tend to be professionals who know many languages. Where there is unemployment, workers worry that migrant labor from other EU countries may make it even harder to find jobs. There is therefore sometimes pressure on governments to limit free movement of labor; after the new Eastern European countries joined in 2004, 12 EU countries required special work permits or made quotas to limit workers from new European member states. Only Britain, Ireland, and Sweden allowed Easterners full access to jobs right away.

## FREE MOVEMENT OF CAPITAL

Capital, or wealth in the form of money or property, can also move easily across borders within Europe now. Businesses can combine across countries, with two companies from different countries merging into one big one. In many countries of Europe, there is a concern that businesses (and therefore jobs) will move to some of the newer Eastern European countries, where it is cheaper to hire workers and conduct business. Some countries are also trying to defend some of their larger, more important companies in sectors such as energy and banking from being taken over by companies based in other countries.

The EU encourages the formation of dynamic companies. It also tries to prevent monopolies, large firms that control a whole sector of production, from forming and extremely large companies from abusing their market power.

## A SINGLE CURRENCY: THE EURO

The creation of a single currency was another way of creating a single market. Since January 2002, more than 300 million Europeans have been using the euro as a normal part of their everyday lives. It replaced currencies that were old symbols of national state power and sovereignty. Businesses can tell more easily how much things actually cost them and how to price things, and they do not have to worry about exchange rates and how they might fluctuate. With the euro, people can travel and shop throughout most of the EU without having to change currency. Of the 15 member states in the Union in 2002, all except Britain, Sweden, and Denmark use the euro. Of the newer members, Slovenia has joined, and Cyprus and Malta joined in January 2008. The euro is probably now the world's second most important currency after the U.S. dollar.

In order to join the euro, countries must show they are following certain rules about their money and government spending. After becoming part of the Eurozone, countries are also supposed to follow certain rules. The European Central Bank, rather than the central banks of individual countries, controls the euro currency.

## PROTECTION FOR ITS CITIZENS

The ability of business to move may increase hardship for certain workers or regions. The area between Paris, London, and Amsterdam is called the "Golden Triangle." With concentrations of technology, skilled workers, and transportation and communication facilities, this has been a strong economic growth area. But other regions have lost traditional industries

Controlled by the European Central Bank, the euro has replaced many national currencies, like the French franc and the Italian lira. The first conversions were made in 2002, changing the coins and bills of 12 individual countries into one common currency.

like textiles, shipping, and steelmaking, or farms. As the single market has developed, the EU has strengthened the funds, called Structural Funds, designed to help these areas.

The EU member states also have social protection or social benefits that help workers who lose jobs or cannot find paid work. Most of these policies are set by individual nation states rather than the EU. There are programs that retrain workers, pay social protection benefits when they are unemployed, and ensure basic income and services. All European countries provide every citizen with health care, unlike the United States, which leaves millions without health insurance.

In the EU, families with children automatically get money that helps them provide food, shelter, and other basics. These benefits have helped people accept the tumult that market competition creates. The EU sees itself as a "fair and caring society." Even the poorest EU members spend more as a percentage of GDP on "social protection" than other wealthy democracies such as the United States and Japan, and overall, the EU has lower percentages of people in poverty than the United States.

The EU has basic employment rules that protect workers in all EU countries. Health and safety laws protect workers against chemical, physical, and biological agents, such as lead and asbestos; prohibit dangerously heavy lifting; and disallow long working hours. Part-time workers and short-term workers, a growing part of the workforce in Europe as well as the United States, also enjoy protections. Individual countries and agreements between unions and companies can make these protections stronger, but they cannot be weaker than the EU minimum. Since the 1970s, the EU has adopted 13 laws on treating women and men equally in hiring, training, promotion, and pay and benefits. It has strengthened its laws against discrimination in the workplace based upon race, ethnicity, national origin, and sexual orientation. There are also laws that guarantee rights for mothers and fathers to stay at home with very young children without losing their jobs.

## GROWTH AND COMPETITION TODAY

European economies grew fast in the 1950s and 1960s, more slowly in the 1970s and 1980s, and even more slowly during the 1990s. Unemployment rates—the percentages of people who are willing and able to work but cannot find jobs—also rose. Meeting in Lisbon in March 2000, the European Council set a new and ambitious goal for the EU: to become, within a decade, the most competitive and dynamic knowledge-based economy in the world, capable of sustainable growth with

Tens of thousands of European workers descended on downtown Brussels as part of the Europe-wide March Against Unemployment in 1997. Protestors in many parts of Europe have argued that the EU has not done enough to protect jobs, as global competition takes its toll.

more and better jobs and greater social cohesion and respect for the environment.[15] They were especially aware that Europe was falling behind the U.S. economy in critical respects and that the economies of China and India posed new global challenges. Leaders identified five areas in which to try to concentrate their efforts:

- Increase science and technology related to the economy

- Continue to develop the free movement of goods, services, and wealth and make the EU a single market
- Make it easier to operate and start businesses
- Increase the percentages of women and older people available for work and encourage people to keep learning over their lifetimes
- Focus on new environmentally friendly products and ways of operating businesses

Because many of these areas are under the control of individual member states, this project was partly a voluntary process involving coordination of national state and European policies. More than halfway through the 10-year period, the results of the Lisbon strategies are not impressive. Growth has inched upward the last few years to about 2.9 percent in the area overall. In the EU, unemployment is highest in Poland at about 17 percent and lowest in Ireland at just over 4 percent of all people who are looking for work. Of the countries in the Eurozone, the average is just over 8 percent.

The EU continues to insist that more free trade and competition will lead to more growth and prosperity. The EU Commission estimates that from 1993 to the present, improving the single market created 2.5 million extra jobs and more than 800 billion euros in extra wealth.[16] But trade within Europe is shrinking in both manufactured goods and services, even though most new jobs are created in the service sector. EU leaders emphasize the importance to business of one set of regulations; better electronic communication, transportation, and energy sources; and the same prices for the same goods and services from one end of the continent to the other.

The EU countries are also examining their systems of social and employment protection to see if there are ways of protecting people without imposing a lot of expenses on companies or slowing down necessary changes in the economy. A large group of political and business leaders in Europe says that states must cut back on social benefits like health care and retirement

## AN AMERICAN COMPANY IN THE EU

Wright Medical Technology Inc. is a medium-size U.S. company, with about 700 employees at its headquarters just outside Memphis, Tennessee. The company designs, makes, and sells products that help replace or restore damaged joints, tissues, and skin. Their knee, hip, elbow, and shoulder joint replacements are made from metals. Surgeons use Wright's special putties made with calcium sulfate to help broken bones mend. These products are referred to as medical devices. Wright also sells thin sheets of material made from cadaver skin that can cover and help heal wounds.

Medical devices are a big, complex, quickly changing sector of industry, with a big impact upon people's health. The European market for medical devices is the world's second largest, after the United States. Europe spends about 41 billion euros on about 8,000 different kinds of medical devices.* With the help of a special unit called Wright Medical Europe, Wright sells about 30 percent of its products, or $100 million of products, in the EU market. Wright employs about 280 people in Europe at seven different locations. Because European people and governments view health care as a basic right, governments own many hospitals, offer or regulate insurance, and try to control costs. Wright's medical devices, like other medical products, tend to bring lower prices in Europe than in the United States.

The existence of the euro, the single currency used by 15 EU countries, has improved Wright's ability to sell their products in Europe. They do not have to think about how to price their products in 15 different currencies or how to take into account how those different currencies change in value relative to the U.S. dollar. It has pensions that raise costs for businesses. They also argue that it must become easier to hire and fire workers. Other groups oppose these ideas, saying that it is essential that economies protect working people and recognize basic rights to well-being

eliminated the costs of constantly changing currencies back and forth. Rather than writing bills in many different currencies, Wright can send all their bills in euros. With a single currency, Wright can see and compare how much they are spending to distribute and market their products in different countries.

Governments carefully regulate medical devices to ensure that they are safe and that the human immune system will not reject them. Very long processes of approval, with lots of different tests, much paperwork, and many meetings, can slow the speed at which new products can be introduced and marketed to hospitals and surgeons. Requirements can be barriers to trade if they are higher in some countries than others. Before 1998, Wright Medical had to get each of its products approved in each country. This could require a lot of energy over a long period of time. In 1998, the EU issued a Medical Device Directive that made things easier. One body acting on behalf of the EU can approve a device for marketing and use through- out the European Union. A positive review earns a new device a CE mark. The letters CE are initials for a French phrase, "Conformité Européenne," or European Conformity, indicating that the product conforms to, or meets, European laws. Some of the products that Wright makes, such as those containing human tissue, still need to be approved country-by-country, according to each country's own pro- cess and requirements.

* "Medical Devices: Regulatory Framework Sound, but Could Be Better Implemented, Says Commission," July 2, 2003. Available online at *http:// europa.eu.int/rapid/pressReleasesAction.do?reference=IP/03/934&format=HTML.*

and to careful procedures in hiring and firing. The British and Irish, for example, offer less social protection for workers, arguing that more work and flexibility are good for growth. The French, Germans, and Swedes, on the other hand, do more to protect workers.

# Food, Agriculture, and Environment

At the end of World War II, farms in Europe were in terrible shape. In the Netherlands, dikes were destroyed. Dikes had been built over centuries to protect low-lying land from the sea and make farming possible. All over the continent, tanks and soldiers had destroyed farmland. Hungry soldiers had eaten everything they could find. Nearly all tractors had been destroyed. Both during and right after the war, governments had to limit adults and children to certain amounts of food per week so that there would be enough for everyone. Europe had to import 40 percent of its food from the United States.[17]

Even as the countryside began to recover, Europe was a mosaic of small-scale farms with each country protecting its own agriculture. Farmers were still exposed to the risks of bad weather and crop and animal disease. Most of them worked very hard for little income, even though they grew food for the whole population. When the EU founders wrote a common agricultural policy into the Treaty of Rome in 1957, they wanted to ensure that Europe could feed itself, that people could find food at affordable prices, and that farmers would have a fair standard of living. These goals would be accomplished through European Economic Community (EEC) policies that applied equally in all EEC countries and that involved European-level funding.

## THE COMMON AGRICULTURAL POLICY (CAP)

The Common Agricultural Policy (CAP) at first involved guaranteeing a high price for farmers for their agricultural goods. To keep the price high, special organizations would buy and store goods. This would create artificial scarcity of supply, and with demand constant or growing, the prices would rise. This is called price support. Under this system, farmers knew that they would get paid for all that they farmed, whether or not consumers wanted to buy it. Also, tariffs were set up for each product coming from outside the EU. By 1968, with the help of CAP, European agriculture had thoroughly recovered from the war and was a big exporter of agricultural goods. France was the world's second-largest exporter of agricultural and food products.

In fact, CAP encouraged farmers to produce too much. To support prices paid to the farmer, some products were stored at great expense. People talked about some of these extras or surpluses as "wine lakes" and "butter mountains." Sometimes these surpluses were sold on the world market at prices below what they actually cost to produce. These cheap exports hurt third-world farmers who could not sell their goods for such low prices. Today, EU farmers get some money to support their income, but they do not get paid according to the total amount they produce. The EU is trying to get agriculture to respond more to demand for food in the market. Some farmers are even rewarded for setting aside land without farming it.

The member states have often disagreed about what sorts of policies the EU should follow in agriculture. France has always benefited from and supported subsidies and tariffs. Fewer than 5 percent of working people in France make their living on the land, but farming still covers about 50 percent of its land surface, and farmers are well organized.[18] Rural life and traditional high-quality food are important in French culture. In addition to France, the countries of Spain, Ireland, and sometimes Germany have fought for keeping tariffs and subsidies. Britain, Sweden, and the Netherlands have wanted change. The new member countries have relatively large agricultural sectors—farms account for about 19 percent of working people in Poland, for example.[19] CAP now takes up about 50 percent of the EU budget, and the new member states with their large agricultural sectors may make it even more costly. The common tariff on agricultural imports and subsidies to certain crops are big issues in international trade. Most final decisions about CAP, involving compromises among countries, are made in the Council of Agricultural Ministers, but the commission plays a major role.

Paying high prices for whatever was produced encouraged farmers to use all available land and produce as much as possible, by using a lot of chemical fertilizers or special animal feed. The farmers who produced more crops or animals got paid more. Their farms grew while smaller farms, which could not compete, closed. Producing a lot of one thing, such as soybeans, often meant lower costs than producing many things, such as vegetables and grains, so farmers specialized.

Specialized, intensive farming created environmental problems. Farming only one particular plant or animal creates a greater likelihood of disease spreading and soil becoming exhausted or polluted. Using too much artificial fertilizer pollutes groundwater and nearby streams. When smaller farms such as olive groves or Alpine pastures are abandoned, their special habitats that support certain kinds of birds and plants

The European Economic Community enacted a Common Agricultural Policy (CAP) in order to help European agriculture recover from its destruction in World War II. Since then, CAP has been reformed several times. In 2002, farmers from France, Ireland, and other countries who relied on subsidies and tariffs protested changes.

disappear. The EU now tries to help the environment by offering aid to farmers who reduce the number of animals per unit of land, leave unplanted fields at the edge of their farms, create ponds, and plant more trees and hedges. Payments to farmers are now made only when farmers take good care of animals, abide by environmental and food safety standards, and contribute to the improvement of the ecology of the countryside.

## FOOD AND ANIMAL SAFETY

The EU has begun to listen to concerns that big, intensive, one-crop or single-animal farms do not produce safe, nutritious, and good-tasting food. Not only did the EU change how they paid farmers, but they also made other policies. Germany played a leading role in trying to improve food quality as well as environmental sensitivity.

Today, EU food-safety rules apply "from farm to fork." The EU makes rules about the safety of both human food and the food fed to animals. It takes into account scientific advice when it does this. It requires that companies disclose the ingredients in food to consumers.

The EU also emphasizes food quality. Farmers can get extra payments if they convert to organic farming. Organic farming keeps soil fertile, has a high standard of animal welfare, avoids all use of artificial additives to soil or animal feed, and prohibits genetically modified organisms (organisms created by putting the genes of one species into another). EU rules make sure that only organic products are labeled organic. New beef-cattle identification systems and meat-labeling rules allow people to trace meat from the store back to the farm where it originated.

In the EU, the animals from which food comes must be healthy. Preventing outbreaks of contagious animal diseases is a high priority, especially after some bad outbreaks of disease in the last decade. EU rules provide for humane methods of rearing, transporting, and slaughtering animals. Research shows that farm animals are healthier and produce better food if they are well treated and able to behave naturally. For

## GMOs IN FOOD

Genetically modified organisms (GMOs) involve taking genes from one species and placing them in another. A lot of big companies have been investing in genetically modified crops. GMOs may make crops such as soybeans, corn, and cotton resistant to insect pests, disease, or drought and therefore attractive to farmers. On the other hand, buying GMO seeds might be more expensive for farmers than using their own seeds or traditional seeds. Scientists are concerned that GMOs might have unknown consequences in the human body and might make certain bacteria resistant to antibiotics.

The EU has adopted a precautionary principle for GMOs. It says that regulators should err on the side of caution and that, until GMOs are proven to be safe, they should not be allowed. The EU examines every case of GMO use. It has not approved many products containing GMOs for sale, and all food products containing GMOs have to be clearly labeled.

In Europe, 54 percent of people consider genetically modified foods dangerous. In the United States, people do not seem as concerned about GMOs, which are in products such as Wheaties cereal. U.S. companies do not even have to label genetically modified foods. U.S. trade negotiators are angry that the EU will not let U.S. GMO products on the shelves. They say there is no scientific basis for barring the products and that they should not be barred unless a danger is proven. They claim that saying no to GMOs is an unfair trade barrier between the United States and Europe. Once, U.S. president George W. Bush said to visiting European leaders,

example, chickens allowed to roam and peck are healthier and, in the end, tastier than hens kept crowded in confinement sheds and fed special foods and drugs that make them grow faster.

**A Greenpeace activist dressed as a mouse holds a handful of genetically modified peas while protesting outside the European Council building in Belgium.**

"Let's go and eat some genetically modified food for lunch," as he led them to the White House dining room.[*]

[*] "Crop Resistance: Why a Transatlantic Split Persists over Genetically Modified Food," *Financial Times*, February 1, 2006. Available online at *http://pewagbiotech.org/newsroom/summaries/display.php3?NewsID=988*.

## PROTECTING THE ENVIRONMENT

When the Treaty of Rome was signed in 1957, there was little awareness of the dangers of environmental pollution and destruction. Farms had not yet grown very large and intensive. Cities had not grown as full of buildings, buses and cars, and factories as they were in 1980. People had not yet formed groups to work for the environment. In the 1970s and 1980s, terrible environmental accidents made Europeans think harder about how economic activity could threaten human health and nature. In 1976, a chemical explosion at Seveso near Milan, Italy, released a dioxin gas cloud which spread, injuring many people and causing choloracne, a serious skin disease, in children. It also killed many animals and plants. In 1978, an oil tanker, the Amoco Cadiz, wrecked off the coast of France and lost 68 million gallons of oil, destroying 110 miles of coastline. In April 1986, a nuclear power plant at Chernobyl in the Ukraine, then part of the Soviet Union, exploded. There were about 30 immediate deaths and many more long-term consequences, such as higher cancer rates in the area, due to radiation contamination. A plume of radioactive fallout drifted over parts of the western Soviet Union, Eastern Europe, Scandinavia, the United Kingdom, and the eastern United States. Only six months after, in November 1986, a fire in a chemical warehouse in Switzerland resulted in tons of toxic chemicals being washed into the Rhine River that runs through Germany, France, Luxembourg, and the Netherlands. Europeans began to understand the fragility of the environment and the particular threats to it in an area of the world that was industrialized and densely populated.

The Single European Act signed in 1987 gave the EU power to preserve, protect, and improve the environment, improve human health, and ensure a good use of natural resources. Later treaties extended these powers. The EU member states had begun to recognize that environmental

*(continues on page 78)*

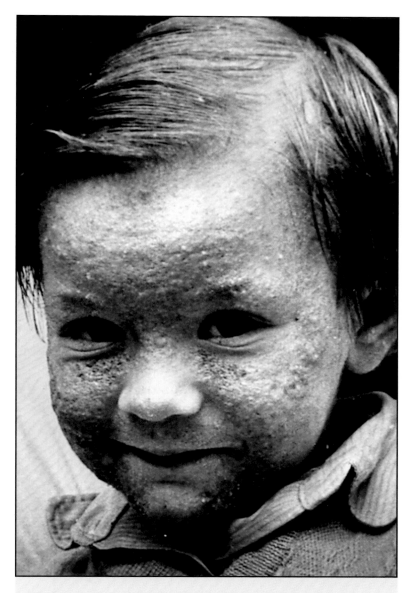

After a series of industrial disasters, the EU set goals and policies in an attempt to decrease damage to human health and the environment. Four-year-old Alice Senno, seen here in 1976, was hospitalized after developing sores caused by a poisonous cloud of chemicals that floated into her Italian village from an accident at Seveso.

# THE BLACK TRIANGLE

Anna Ljtarova, age 51 and with three daughters, said, "We moved in June 1984 from a clean, unpolluted area of the country, and by October my health began to deteriorate. I had pneumonia and bronchitis during the winter, terrible allergies with watery, puffy eyes during the summer and horrible red rashes over my whole body. It was a nightmare.... After several years my windpipe began to contract and I could hardly breathe at times. There is nothing more terrifying."* She was describing the health effects of living in the "Black Triangle."

The Black Triangle is the name given to the area where Poland, Germany, and the Czech Republic come together. Under the Communist regimes in these countries, pollution problems were neglected because the priority was developing industry and making industrial goods. It was one of Europe's most heavily industrialized and heavily polluted regions. For many decades, choking coal dust given off by power plants and all kinds of discharges from the industries in the area plagued the Black Triangle.

The main source of pollution in the area was lignite, a soft type of coal abundant in the area. When lignite is burned to create electrical power or heat, it gives off soot, ash, dust, dangerous metals, and sulfur and nitrogen oxides. Sulfur and nitrogen oxides combine with moisture in the air to create "acid rain," a substance that kills trees and animals and corrodes buildings. The presence of lignite, a cheap source of fuel, attracted industry to the Black Triangle.

The pollution in the Black Triangle sickened more than half a million people. Respiratory disease was very common, allergies were widespread, and heart disease and cancer were above average for the countries. Even though things have now improved, children in the area are much sicker than average.

After the end of Communism, since 1991, the environment ministers of the three Black Triangle countries have been working together to develop a cross-boundary plan to reduce pollution. The

**Dirty plumes of air rise from power plants in the Czech Republic.**

European Commission joined as a partner. Some progress has come from shutting down old industries, but people have also found ways of burning lignite more efficiently and without releasing as many pollutants. In one of the cities that had been the most polluted, trees are now healthy, many songbirds have returned, and townspeople have planted a vineyard on land that used to be part of a mine. **

* Don Hinrichsen, "On a Slow Trip Back from Hell," *International Wildlife Magazine*, January/February 1998. Available online at *http://www.nwf.org/internationalwildlife/1998/triangle.html.*

** Henry Maczyk, "The Black Triangle: Reducing Air Pollution in Central Europe." Available online at *http://www.energy.rochester.edu/pl/blacktriangle/.*

*(continued from page 74)*
problems such as air and river pollution need cooperative problem solving across borders. They also realized
that environmental regulations could affect the costs and
competitiveness of businesses; environmental laws can raise
costs if they are stricter or lower costs if they are weaker. This
would create unfair competition in the single market. EU
leaders also became more concerned about public health and
pollution. By 1993, most environmental laws could be passed
by the council by qualified majority vote and did not have to
be passed unanimously.

The EU passes laws and sets goals in many areas of the
environment. Since the 1990s, it has tended to be cautious
about the environment, trying to take action before damage is
done. The European Commission describes its environmental
priorities as air, water, waste, and nature.

Air is a common resource that does not respect national
boundaries, and so the EU tries to create uniform laws across
all countries about what can be put into the air or how dirty
the air can be overall. One special concern about air quality is
global warming. When people use coal, oil, and gas in factories, transportation, and homes, carbon dioxide is emitted into
the air. Carbon dioxide keeps invisible radiation from being
reflected back out to the atmosphere and traps it close to the
earth, making Earth warmer. Right now, Earth's climate seems
to be warming up too much. Experts think global warming
might cause sea levels to rise and more extreme weather, such
as storms and floods, to appear.

The EU has joined with other countries to try to reduce
emissions of carbon dioxide. It adopted the United Nations
Convention (agreement) on Climate Change and the Kyoto
Protocol. In March 2007, the EU heads of state agreed to a long-
term energy strategy, to be met by 2020, with targets for renew-
able sources (energy sources such as wind and solar power that

do not use limited resources), for biofuels (fuel made from plant materials), and for reductions of damaging carbon emissions that heat the environment. The new energy agenda was widely seen as laying down a challenge to the United States and other industrial countries to take similar action.

Two kinds of water problems, flooding and pollution, are a menace to EU countries. Serious floods in Italy, France, and the United Kingdom are related to the fact that huge parking lots, shopping centers, roads, and intensive farms with heavily packed soil block rainwater's access back to the soil. The biggest water pollution problems are now caused not by industry, which must follow EU rules, but by the use of fertilizers, manure, and pesticides in agriculture and by leaks in underground tanks used to store heating oil. As water comes into contact with these, it carries them into the rivers and then the sea.

Since the 1970s, the EU has also been working on how to manage waste that comes from farms, mining, industry, and households. It encourages reduction of waste, increased recycling, and safe handling of waste within and between countries.

Protection of wildlife and natural habitats (sometimes called biodiversity) is part of environmental policy. In 1979, the EU passed a directive saying that member states must protect wild birds. Since many of the birds were migratory, it was important that Europe act. The 1992 habitats directive protects certain habitats, called Natura 2000 sites.

The largest number of environmental laws control dangerous chemicals and other hazardous substances. Some of these laws are about packaging and labeling. Others restrict the use of hazardous substances or ensure that companies take precautions to prevent accidents and have emergency plans. Some limit the export and import of dangerous substances.

The 10 countries that joined the EU in 2004—Czech Republic, Cyprus, Estonia, Hungary, Latvia, Lithuania, Malta,

Poland, Slovakia, and Slovenia—are important to the environment in the Union. On the one hand, they have great natural environmental wealth; for example, beech forests in the Carpathian Mountains in the Czech Republic, Poland, Hungary, Slovakia, and Romania; wetlands along the Biebrza River in Poland; and a reed system near the Danube River delta in Romania. Farming has not been as intensive in these countries. On the other hand, environmental pollution from industry under Communist regimes was severe, and it will be a challenge for these countries to clean up and implement new standards.

# People and Culture

THE MOTTO OF THE EU IS "UNITY IN DIVERSITY." ONE TYPE OF diversity in the EU is that of the nation state; 27 states now make up the Union. Language differences to a certain extent follow the political boundaries. There are many large and small European ethnic groups, such as Germans, Poles, Welsh, Basques, and Galicians, within the EU. Inside Europe, there are also non-European ethnic groups and cultures, mainly the result of migrations from Africa and Asia since World War II. Among these migrants are many Muslims, who represent a growing minority religious group in Europe. Europe has many types of language, ethnic, and religious diversity, and the EU plays a role in recognizing and managing these differences.

## LANGUAGE AND DIVERSITY

There are more than 200 European languages, and each country in the EU has one or more official languages. An official language is a language that is given a special legal status in a country, state, or other territory. Usually it is the language used by the main nationality or ethnic group. Other languages are often referred to as minority languages.

In the 25 countries that were in the EU in 2004, German is the most widely spoken first language, spoken by 18 percent as a native language, followed by English and Italian at 13 percent, and French at 12 percent. In the EU-25, 56 percent speak a language other than their first language, and 28 percent master two foreign languages. About 38 percent know English, and 14 percent French or German. The enlargement of Europe to the east has shifted the balance between French- and German-language speakers in the EU, as more citizens in the eastern countries speak German. Russian has also become one of the most spoken languages because of its influence in the new Baltic member states of Lithuania, Latvia, and Estonia.[20]

Respect and support for language diversity, including both official and minority languages, have been fundamental to the EU. In the founding Treaty of Rome, the EU said that the official languages of Europe would be the official languages of the member states and that citizens had the right to communicate with the EU institutions in their own languages. Currently, there are 23 officially recognized languages. However, the EU uses English, French, and German more than others for much of its official business. Article 22 of the European Charter of Fundamental Rights says, "The Union respects cultural, religious and linguistic diversity," and Article 21 forbids discrimination based upon language. The EU has an official policy of multilingualism. This means both that it encourages individuals to learn many languages and that it supports the coexistence and interaction of many language communities within Europe. Among organizations of nation states, the EU is unique in the emphasis it puts upon these language issues. There is even a special commissioner for multilingualism.

Some people argue that it is hopelessly complicated and expensive for the EU to use 23 languages and try to get people to learn second and third languages. But the EU says that using many languages is a way to make the Union more accessible and understandable to all its citizens. The EU also says that languages make people more open to the culture of others, enrich

## OFFICIAL LANGUAGES OF THE EU

| LANGUAGE, ABB. | ENGLISH TRANSLATION OF LANGUAGE NAME |
|---|---|
| Español (ES) | Spanish |
| Dansk (DA) | Danish |
| Deutsch (DE) | German |
| Elinika (EL) | Greek |
| English (EN) | |
| Français (FR) | French |
| Italiano (IT) | Italian |
| Nederlands (ND) | Dutch |
| Portugues (PT) | Portuguese |
| Suomi (FI) | Finnish |
| Svenska (SV) | Swedish |
| Cestina (CS) | Czech |
| Eesti (ET) | Estonian |
| Latviesu valoda (LV) | Latvian |
| Lietuviu kalba (LT) | Lithuanian |
| Magyar (HU) | Hungarian |
| Malti (MT) | Maltese |
| Polski (PL) | Polish |
| Slovencina (SK) | Slovak |
| Slovenscina (SL) | Slovene |
| Gaeilge (GA) | Irish |
| Romano (RO) | Romanian |
| Balgarski (BG) | Bulgarian |

their lives, and expand their relationships. Finally, the EU says that it needs multilingual citizens to make its single market a reality and its economy strong. To trade with companies in other member states, European businesses need skills in the languages of the EU. Companies lose business when they cannot speak their customers' languages, and if people are going to work across boundaries of nation states, they need to be able to use languages.

## ETHNIC AND RELIGIOUS BACKGROUNDS

Most European countries developed around a dominant ethnic group. For example, Germany was based on German ethnicity, France on French ethnicity, Poland on Polish ethnicity. These countries have deep historical, cultural, religious, and language traditions. This is different from the United States, a relatively new country originally populated by native peoples and developed by colonial settlers, African slaves, and immigrants. Since World War II, more people have been moving around Europe and the globe to pursue economic opportunities, to escape difficult and terrifying conditions, and to reunite with family members, so immigration and many cultures have become a reality in Europe.

After World War II, countries began recruiting workers from abroad to fill jobs that native workers did not want in Europe's growing economies. France recruited workers from its former colonies in northern Africa—Morocco, Algeria, and Tunisia. The United Kingdom recruited workers from its former colonies in the Caribbean and south Asia. Germany, which had lost its colonies earlier, recruited workers from Turkey. Spanish, Portuguese, and Italian workers also went to these three more prosperous countries. In the 1970s, as jobs became scarcer and politicians and people reacted against immigrants, France, the United Kingdom, and Germany stopped receiving new immigrant workers. Family members hurried to join the immigrants and began to form settled communities. By the

1990s, more people from parts of southeastern Europe, Africa, and the Middle East desperate to flee violence and persecution were coming to Europe, seeking protection. Countries that were not used to immigrants had to adjust to the fact that they were now countries with many different peoples and cultures. Many immigrants were both ethnic minorities and Muslims, a minority religious group in Europe.

In all European countries, ethnic minorities tend to be poorer than the majority group. Minority groups tend to get less education. They often live in poor-quality housing in segregated neighborhoods. From the time they arrived, these minority groups were discriminated against, or treated less favorably compared to others in their same position or with their same qualifications. Today in many countries in Europe, there are political parties that say that immigrants and ethnic minority groups can never fit into society, have inferior cultures, are taking jobs away from the majority ethnic group, and are responsible for increased crime.

Beginning in the late 1960s, some EU member states began passing laws forbidding discrimination based on skin color or ethnic group. Some of these laws also forbade discrimination on the basis of religion, but others did not.

The problem of religious discrimination has been felt especially by Muslims. Muslims now are about 5 percent of the EU population, about 8 percent in France, 4 percent in Germany, and 3 percent in the United Kingdom. Many of the younger generation born in Europe are fairly religious. They may fast during the holy month of Ramadan, attend mosque regularly, eat only meat slaughtered in the correct ritual fashion (halal), and wear certain kinds of traditional headscarves or skullcaps. Most Muslims in Europe live peaceful, ordinary lives. They feel especially vulnerable after terrorists who were Muslim extremists crashed planes into the Twin Towers in New York City and the Pentagon in Washington, D.C., in September

(continues on page 88)

# A WINNING KICK AGAINST RACISM IN SOCCER

Soccer, called football in Europe, is one place that it is easy to see negative attitudes and actions toward ethnic minorities, immigrants, and Jews in Europe. Most soccer fans in Europe are white Europeans, about 20–30 percent of top-level players are black, and there are few black coaches or referees. Disturbing incidents have occurred in many countries. Black players for England, Germany, and the Netherlands have been subjected to monkey noises and scratching motions and racist slurs. Rival fans regularly make hissing noises supposed to represent Nazi gas chambers against teams that used to be associated with Jewish neighborhoods or business sponsors. Soccer fans writing to newspapers defend these actions, saying "fans" are just rooting for their teams. The sports governing bodies, politicians, coaches, and antiracism groups are alarmed; they say a soccer stadium is a place where people can anonymously say things that are generally unacceptable and have their ideas confirmed.

Many people and organizations have fought back against soccer racism. UEFA is the organization that runs professional soccer in Europe. Its president has said, "Racism is unquestionably one of the most abject forms of disrespect towards fellow human beings. It has no place in our society and even less so in team sports like football, where all members of the team are equally important when it comes to achieving the desired result."* UEFA has helped set up a group called Football Against Racism in Europe (FARE). UEFA has had large antiracism conferences with soccer stars and political leaders from across countries and the EU. Members of the EU Parliament have made a declaration against soccer racism backed by UEFA that calls on referees to stop or abandon matches in the event of serious racist abuse. Here is part of their statement:

It is a sad reflection on our world that racism continues to blight the beautiful game. Football is not the cause of racism,

Before the start of a German soccer match, fans hold up red cards saying, "Award the red card to racism." A red card is a serious soccer penalty.

but it is in our stadiums and on our pitches that some of the most visible and violent abuses take place. We should see this as an opportunity. The massive popularity of football presents us with the means to reach millions of people and, we must hope, to promote tolerance and understanding. . . . In the world of football . . . each member of the family—the associations, leagues, clubs, players, referees and supporters—has its role to play. Our declaration calls for a joint effort from everyone that cares about football. **

* "United Against the Racists," UEFA.com, January 17, 2006. Available online at *http://www.uefa.com/news/newsid=385888.htm.*

** "Written Declaration of the European Parliament on Tackling Racism in Football," December 9, 2005. Available online at *http://www.enar-eu.org/anti-racism-diversity-intergroup/activities/Declaration69.*

*(continued from page 85)*
2001; bombed trains in Madrid, Spain, in March 2004; and attacked buses and subways in London in July 2005.

Article 13 of the 1997 Treaty of Amsterdam gave the European Community the powers to fight discrimination on the grounds of sex, race/ethnic origin, religion/belief, disability, age, and sexual orientation. In 2000, the European Community enacted an important law, called the Racial Equality Directive, that outlawed discrimination based on race and ethnic origin. A separate law, called the Employment Framework Directive, applies to employment and occupations. It prohibits discrimination at work on the grounds of religion, political belief, disability, age, or sexual orientation. (The EU already had a lot of laws against sex discrimination.) As a result of these two laws, many member states had to strengthen their own laws against discrimination. In addition, in 2000, the EU adopted a document called the Charter of Fundamental Rights. It sets out in one place all the rights of European citizens, and it includes many rights to equal treatment. The EU also creates other programs to try to fight discrimination, especially in areas related to work and business.

## THE CHARTER OF FUNDAMENTAL RIGHTS OF THE EUROPEAN UNION

### Article 21 Non-discrimination

Any discrimination based on any ground such as sex, race, color, ethnic or social origin, genetic features, language, religion or belief, political or any other opinion, membership of a national minority, property, birth, age, disability, or sexual orientation should be prohibited.

### Article 22 Cultural, religious and linguistic diversity

The Union shall respect cultural, religious and linguistic diversity.

The EU member states also limit the entry of non-Europeans into EU countries. While the borders inside Europe are weakening, the border around the perimeter of the EU is strengthening. Some people call it "Fortress Europe"; the immigration barriers for people from Africa, Asia, the Middle East, and Latin America are high and strong. Rules about immigration from outside Europe are still under the control of the member states. But the EU is trying to establish some common principles about certain types of immigration and trying to reduce all forms of illegal immigration.

Illegal immigration occurs when people try to come into a country without following procedures set out in law. Sometimes they are so desperate they endanger their lives. A major issue in Europe is illegal immigration from Africa, especially via the Strait of Gibraltar, where thousands of people die every year in attempts to reach Europe. About a million illegal immigrants from Africa live and work illegally in southern Spain. For many years, desperate refugees being held in Sangatte in northern France would try to use the tunnel under the English Channel, a 35-mile-long tunnel with train tracks and a highway, to escape their refugee center and get to a better life in England. About 1,000 a month were caught, and several were killed after being hit by trains or by electrocution. Sometimes illegal immigration into Europe is organized by smugglers, who take money from immigrants or from people who want to use the cheap labor of illegal immigrants, or both.

Another difficult issue is asylum. Most governments have agreed that refugees, people outside their own country and at risk of harm due to their beliefs or who they are, should be offered asylum, or protection, in other countries. European countries recognize the right to asylum, but they vary in how they decide if someone is really a refugee in danger and under what conditions they can stay. The European Commission is

While the EU tries to develop some common guidelines for immigrants coming from outside the Union, most member states are trying to limit illegal immigration. Here, a group of 106 African immigrants in a small boat trying to enter Spain is stopped by authorities.

trying to coordinate asylum procedures, bringing together 27 different laws into one set of guidelines.

## EUROPEAN MINORITIES

European nation states have been built around dominant ethnic groups, but things have always been more complicated. There have been many minority ethnic groups living in Europe itself, speaking their own languages and having a distinct set of traditions. These groups include the Basques who inhabit parts of both Spain and France; Galicians who live in the Spanish regions of Asturias and Castile; the Sudeten German ethnic and linguistic minority in the Czech Republic; the Welsh, who are concentrated in the region of Wales in the United Kingdom;

and many others. In the 1990s, European countries, including but beyond the EU, drew up legal documents protecting national minorities and their languages.

The largest ethnic minority in Europe is the Roma people. The Roma are also called Travellers or Gypsies. About 10 million Roma live in Europe as a whole, a population larger than the population of some EU member states. A lot of Roma live in Eastern Europe, so the Roma population in the EU increased when these new states joined in 2004.

The Roma originally migrated from the Indian subcontinent to Europe around A.D. 1000. Their language, Romani, originated in the area of India, and they tend to live in tight-knit, big families; they often travel rather than settle down in one place. Roma music is famous for quick-playing, sometimes tragically sad violins, small mandolins, drums, and wooden spoons. Like most large cultural groups, the Roma are diverse; they speak different dialects of their language, have different customs and traditions, and are both Christian and Muslim. In previous centuries, they were enslaved in some areas, and children were removed from families and communities. They were systematically killed by the Germans in World War II. Since the end of World War II, they have been forced to settle in certain places, been prevented from having children, had their children taken away from them, and been segregated into separate schools.

Today, Roma have very low levels of education, have a lot of difficulty finding jobs, live in substandard housing separated from other groups, have high levels of contagious illnesses such as tuberculosis, and die younger than other groups. They are often not treated fairly by legal systems, employers, schools, and people supposed to give them social protection. When the new member states were about to join the EU in 2004, some experts said that these countries violated the basic human rights of the Roma so much that they did not meet the Copenhagen criterion for joining the EU of "a stable democracy respecting

The Roma, also referred to as Gypsies or Travellers, are the largest ethnic minority group in Europe, and also one of the poorest. The Roma
face discrimination in employment, housing, and social services, and
Roma children generally have problems getting a good education.

human rights, the rule of law and the protection of minorities." Before allowing new countries to join, the EU worked
in partnership with the new countries applying for membership to try to improve the human rights and social conditions
of the Roma. Many current EU laws and special programs
address the problems of the Roma.

# The EU On
# the World Stage

COUNTRIES IN EUROPE ARE CONNECTED IN MANY WAYS to faraway regions of the globe, such as Africa, Asia, and the Middle East. For example, trade extends not only between neighboring countries, such as France and Germany, but also between Europe and China. Armed conflict and violence in African countries create migrants and refugees who seek asylum in Europe. New forms of information technology, such as the Internet and satellites, allow Europeans to see and understand what is happening far away. They can see, for example, whether severe poverty and war are shortening the lives of children in Africa or whether political leaders or armed rebels are violating basic human rights in Latin America. Of course the European continent is not the only area of the world that is experiencing more interconnections and interdependencies with other regions of the world. This increasing linkage between what is happening in one place and what is happening in far-off places is called globalization. The EU therefore is not only active in Europe itself but is also a player on the world stage.

## AN ECONOMIC GIANT

Today, the EU is an economic superpower. It has 7 percent of the world's population but about 30 percent of the world's gross domestic product. It is the world's biggest trader. It exports more than 38 percent of all the exports in the world. With a wealthy population of 450 million, it is the biggest market in the industrialized world. About a third of the corporations on the list of the largest 100 industrial corporations in 2000 were based in Europe. They included car companies, such as DaimlerChrysler, Volkswagen, and Fiat, and two oil companies, Royal Dutch Shell and BP Amoco.[21]

Consistent with its own positive experience bringing down trade barriers in its internal market, the EU generally favors free trade among all countries. The World Trade Organization (WTO) makes rules about international trade and tries to bring down tariffs and other barriers so that the world becomes more of a free-trade zone. As a member of the WTO that speaks with a single voice, the EU tries to pressure countries to lower tariff barriers. The EU's average tariff on industrial imports has now fallen to 4 percent, one of the lowest in the world.[22] However, the EU still protects the livelihood of its farmers with tariffs and subsidies (extra government payments to producers). This makes it harder for smaller farmers in developing countries to sell what they farm, because, with the extra tariff, their goods are more expensive in Europe and fewer people buy them. Or, if rich countries give extra money to farmers to help pay their bills, their farmers can charge buyers less and still take in enough money. Cameroon in West Africa depends upon selling its cotton, but sales suffer partly because both the EU and the United States give subsidies to their cotton farmers.

Global free trade depends not only on lowering tariffs but also on lowering nontariff barriers to trade. These can include subsidies and certain government monopolies (when the government owns or operates a certain service and does not let private companies do so at the same time). Global trade negotiations also have moved from considering only industrial and agricultural products to making rules about other things. Trade in services raises interesting questions: For example, can doctors or nurses trained in one country practice freely in another? There are also rules about cultural products; for example, can a country protect its small movie industry? Ideas and techniques for making things also raise questions; for example, who owns the formula for lifesaving drugs and who can make and sell cheaper copies of these drugs? The EU has been involved in these kinds of international trade negotiations, too.

The EU and the United States are important trading partners. They are the two biggest economies in the world. The United States receives about 24 percent of EU exports and supplies 18 percent of EU imports. Twelve to 14 million jobs in the EU and the United States depend on trade between Europe and the United States. Disputes between the United States and Europe break out from time to time. A number of these disputes are settled directly between the two countries. Some go through a special WTO process that settles disputes. The United States challenged the EU's decision to keep out meat from cattle treated with growth hormones, certain substances that make animals grow faster. The United States challenged EU rules about importing bananas. And the EU challenged the United States' decision to put a 30 percent tariff on steel imports from a majority of the rest of the world. These disputes make headlines, but they represent only about 2 percent of total U.S.-EU trade.[23]

The EU's trade policy is closely linked to its historic ties with former colonies and its interest in helping these countries become stronger economies and democracies. In the past, the EU had special agreements with these former colonies, called the African, Caribbean and Pacific states (ACP). In 1975, 46 countries in these three world regions were included in the official grouping. The EU offered tariff-free access for many products, mainly foods and minerals, without asking these smaller states to allow EU products free access. This meant that the EU was actually helping producers in these smaller states to sell more in Europe while still allowing those countries to protect their own farmers and other economic activities.

In 2000, the EU and 77 developing countries signed a new agreement to reduce poverty through trade and other means. It was signed at Cotonou in the African country of Benin. This agreement covered a sixth of the world population. The long-term plan for trade is to create free trade with no tariff barriers or quotas for all countries. The EU promised to lower barriers but so must the ACP countries. For the 49 poorest countries in the world, the EU in 2001 promised tariff-free entry into the EU for all their exports—with the sole exception of arms and ammunition. In 2003, about 80 percent of poor countries' exports entered the EU with no or reduced tariffs.[24] This helps poorer countries whose goods remain at lower prices than if they had a tax or tariff imposed on them when they came into the country. These goods have a better chance of competing successfully and bringing more income to producers in poorer countries. The Cotonou agreement said a lot about trade but also emphasized democratic politics, human rights, rules of law, absence of government corruption, and peace. It said that equality between men and women and good practices toward the environment were important. It encouraged countries to pursue free trade with their neighbors.

The EU works to realize the United Nations Millennium Development Goals adopted in 2000. These goals are to eradicate extreme hunger and poverty; to give every child a good primary school education; to strengthen equality between girls and boys, men and women; to reduce the deaths of infants; to improve the health of mothers; to combat HIV/AIDS, malaria, and other diseases; to protect the environment; and to create partnerships between countries and organizations for development.

The EU is a player on the global, not just the European, stage. It works closely with other countries and international organizations. Here, children hold a giant AIDS ribbon at a March 2007 conference on combating AIDS in Africa and around the world.

The EU and its member states combined are the largest donor for overseas development assistance, but they do not yet give 0.7 percent of their GDP—a goal first proposed by a Canadian in 1969 that Europe is reaching for by 2015. Five countries in Europe—Sweden, Luxembourg, Norway, the Netherlands, and Denmark—exceed that percentage. (The United States gives 0.16 percent of its GDP.)

## HUMANITARIAN ASSISTANCE AND POST-CONFLICT RECONSTRUCTION

At 11:00 A.M. London time on January 4, 2005, much of Europe observed three minutes of silence. Cars stopped in the streets of Stockholm, Sweden; noisy stock traders in Germany stopped buying and selling stocks; mourning crowds stood shoulder to shoulder in the center of Paris; televisions went silent in the United Kingdom. This silence was a small way to remember the 200,000 people killed by the Asian tsunami on December 26, 2004. The big sea wave that hit countries around the Indian Ocean was one of the worst natural disasters in recorded history. In Indonesia, the coastal areas of Aceh and North Sumatra were destroyed. By the time of the big silence across Europe, the EU, individual countries, and European charities had begun to pledge assistance to the Indonesian communities.

 ## BANANAS

People in the EU eat a lot of bananas, and the EU imports about a third of the world's traded bananas. Bananas in St. Lucia, St. Vincent, Dominica, Grenada (called the Windward Islands), and some parts of Jamaica are produced on small family farms in hilly areas. In the Windward Islands, bananas produce over half of all export earnings and are vital to the economy. These small economies had been British colonies and were part of the African, Caribbean and Pacific states (ACP). "Dollar bananas," on the other hand, are associated with big U.S. corporations such as Dole, Del Monte, and Chiquita. They are grown in Latin American countries such as Ecuador, Costa Rica, and Honduras; those countries also depend upon banana income. The bananas are grown on big, flat plantations, and the costs of growing them are relatively low.

The EU has had a very complicated system of tariffs (import taxes) and quotas (maximum numbers) for banana imports to protect the small banana-dependent economies in the ACP countries. It allowed 858,000 tons of ACP bananas to come in without tariffs. It limited the entry of dollar bananas to about 2.2 million tons a year

From the beginning, the EU played a leading role in the international response to the tsunami. It pledged and sent funds quickly and played a role in coordinating many donors. The EU focused upon both immediate humanitarian relief to the victims and reconstruction of the devastated communities. One EU project, for example, was reconstruction of the fishing village of Lhok Ngok. There, half the population was killed, and most of the fishing boats and equipment were destroyed. EU money went toward building a boat-making yard and fitting some of the newly

with a tariff of about 75 euros per ton. The EU thought that free trade should be balanced by the need for survival in some of the small banana-producing economies.

The United States and five of the Latin American banana-producing countries complained to the World Trade Organization (WTO) that European policy was discriminating against them. In 1997, a WTO body responsible for resolving trade disputes ruled against the EU banana-trade policy. In 2001, the European Commission, the United States, and Ecuador agreed to eliminate quotas on bananas coming from different countries and to use only tariffs. In 2006, the EU imposed a single tariff on all banana imports but kept 775,000 tons tariff-free for ACP countries. But other banana exporters argue that these policies also violate WTO free-trade rules, and negotiations continue.*

---

* Oxfam, "A Future for Caribbean Bananas." Available online at *http://www.oxfam.org.uk/what_we_do/issues/trade/wto_bananas.htm*;

"EU Defeat in Banana Export Battle," BBC News, August 1, 2005. Available online at *http://news.bbc.co.uk/go/pr/fr/-/2/hi/business/4735983.stm.*

built boats with equipment for surviving fishermen. To help the Indonesian and other governments plan for reconstruction, EU specialists took satellite photos of the destroyed coastlines. The EU has participated with other countries in developing an early warning system for tsunamis in the Indian and Atlantic oceans, and the Mediterranean Sea.

Before the tsunami, Aceh had been the place of a bloody struggle. Rebels had fought the Indonesian government to be able to control more resources in their area and receive more recognition of their culture and Islamic religion. Human rights observers said that the Indonesian army had violated the human rights of the rebels—killing, torturing, and imprisoning many of them. After the tsunami, the EU became involved in trying to start peace negotiations and then supervise the peace agreement between the Indonesian government and rebels in Aceh. The EU thought that without peace the province of Aceh would never recover from the destruction of the tsunami. The European Union, Norway, Switzerland, and the Association of Southeast Asian Nations (ASEAN) worked to make sure the peace agreement was being followed. The monitors were all civilians, not soldiers, and about 100 were from the EU. They collected and destroyed the arms turned in by rebel fighters. They made sure that soldiers and armed police from the Indonesian government left the province when the peace agreement said they should. The EU tried to help the rebel fighters return to normal jobs and everyday life. It is trying to support democracy and the rule of law in the area.

Thus, the EU also uses its economic wealth to grant humanitarian assistance to poorer countries. When either natural disaster or armed conflict erupts, it works through the European Community Humanitarian Aid Office (ECHO) and often with the United Nations system, especially the United Nations High Commission on Refugees. It also has developed a specialty in "peace-building"—supporting peace negotiations, contributing to peacekeeping forces, disarming soldiers and returning them

In order to help restore peace and economic livelihoods after the Indian Ocean tsunami of 2004, the EU helped negotiate a peace agreement between the Indonesian government and rebels in Aceh, the hardest-hit region in Indonesia. International organizations and individual countries worked together to build peace, gathering and destroying rebel weapons, and monitoring the government's observance of the peace agreement.

to peaceful jobs, getting rid of land mines (explosive devices on the ground), helping children who have been in war zones, and rebuilding economies in war-damaged areas.

## FOREIGN POLICY

While treaties give the EU power over trade, they only give it limited power to conduct foreign policy, or political relations with other countries. Member states still make a lot of their own policies. This is an area in which the EU does not act like a single sovereign state.

One interesting example of how the European Union does not have a single foreign policy was the controversy over the Iraq War. In 2003, the United States led a war to destroy the dictatorship of Saddam Hussein in Iraq and what it said were its dangerous weapons, which posed a threat to U.S. security. The U.S. president said that Iraq had links with Al Qaeda, which had masterminded the attacks on the Twin Towers and the Pentagon in 2001. However, many EU member states doubted that there was any link between Iraq and the September 11 terrorist attacks on New York City or any evidence that Iraq had weapons of mass destruction (after the war, no such weapons were found). International law says that states can go to war only in self-defense, after being authorized by the United Nations. The EU member states disagreed about whether the United States had followed the rules of the United Nations or whether the United States should get the agreement of the United Nations. All European countries and the United States are members of the UN, an organization that is supposed to bring countries together to make decisions about war and peace.

Germany and France thought that the war was illegal. Even though most of the British people were against the war, Britain, under Prime Minister Tony Blair, said that Saddam Hussein had these weapons and that the United States was right to wage a war against Iraq. Britain sent troops to fight. Leaders of seven other countries in the EU—Spain, Italy, Poland, Hungary, Denmark, Portugal, and the Czech Republic—said they agreed with the

United States. Several former Communist countries in Eastern Europe supported the war. All EU countries, however, support efforts to bring stability to Iraq. Europe has made big contributions to humanitarian relief and reconstructing Iraq after the damage of war. It also provided $24 million to help write the new, democratic Iraqi constitution and channeled this money through the United Nations.

In foreign policy, the EU may not always be unified on issues of war and peace or have its own large army under an EU command. One reason that the EU may not have its own army and defense policy is that the countries of Europe are already covered by another organization, the North Atlantic Treaty Organization, which is led by the United States. The North Atlantic Treaty Organization began in 1949 as a military and political alliance of European countries and North America, designed to protect Western Europe from a Soviet attack. It still exists today as the main military defense organization for Europe and North America.

The EU is working on ways of taking common positions on issues of war and peace in the world. EU foreign policy stresses negotiation rather than war and emphasizes the cooperation of countries based on international law. It also strongly supports the importance of human rights in the world. The EU is affected by Europe's terrible history of destructive war and a wish to avoid war and use of military force where possible. It is also affected by its own success. EU countries that were military rivals have found a way to engage in dialogue and cooperation. The foreign and defense ministers of the member states have decided to use both military and civilian forces for humanitarian, rescue, peacekeeping, peacemaking, and crisis-management jobs, often in cooperation with the United Nations and other international organizations.

# The EU: Past, Present, and Future

THE EU MARKED ITS FIFTIETH ANNIVERSARY IN 2007. In 2007, Bulgaria and Romania joined the EU. Slovenia became the thirteenth country to join the euro currency, and Cyprus and Malta were recommended for Eurozone membership starting January 1, 2008.

Since its founding, the EU has changed almost beyond recognition. It has grown from the original 6 members to include 27, spreading and strengthening democracy and economic prosperity in the process. In the 1970s, Denmark, Ireland, and the United Kingdom joined the original six— Belgium, Germany, France, Italy, Luxembourg, and the Netherlands. The Mediterranean countries of Greece, Spain, and Portugal in the 1980s and the countries of Sweden,

Finland, and Austria in the 1990s further increased membership. Since 2000, 10 formerly Communist countries have joined, marking an end to the Cold War division of Europe.

The scourge of war between EU members has been avoided. The idea of the founders was that new institutions of cooperation would help leaders think in terms of interests that went beyond the individual nation state and so dampen their rivalry. There was also an idea that countries that traded with each other would be less likely to go to war. As Europe has grown, it has continued to emphasize the importance of democracy and peaceful negotiation of differences. There has been war on the continent of Europe and elsewhere in the world, but not among the EU member states.

Today, Europe is much more than just a common market without tariff barriers. The EU quickly became a customs union, abolishing tariffs on trade among member states and creating a common set of tariffs on imports from countries outside Europe. It has continued to work on making the European Union not only a free-trade area but also a single market. Work on the "four freedoms" of movement—goods, labor, wealth, and services—intensified in the 1980s and 1990s. In 2002, 12 member states adopted a common currency, under the control of a European Central Bank. Because of all this, citizens of EU member states are free to work, travel, and study anywhere in the Union. The EU's powers to create a single market have led to policymaking in many areas related to the market, such as the environment, consumer protection, health and safety, and equality and nondiscrimination at work.

The EU has also become a political actor on the world stage. It is a major contributor of development assistance to poorer countries. It is a leader in tackling international climate change. The EU has participated in international peacemaking in many places and sent troops to countries in Asia and Africa.

Three large questions remain. How big can the EU become? Do ordinary people really support it? Is the EU creating economic prosperity?

## SIZE

French and Dutch voters may have rejected the new EU Constitution partly because they thought that Europe was expanding too fast, and even some EU member states disagree about the desirability of Turkish membership in the Union. Some people are eager to admit the western Balkan countries—Croatia, Bosnia and Herzegovina, Albania, Montenegro, Serbia, and Macedonia—and some independent countries that used to be part of the Soviet Union—Moldova, Ukraine, and Belarus. If Europe is not merely a geographical location but a set of political and economic ideas and ways of doing things, where are its boundaries? Can the institutions work with so many member states and peoples?

## SUPPORT OF THE PEOPLE

Political leaders rather than the people themselves devised the EU. The ideas of Jean Monnet and Robert Schuman were critical to launching the EU, and for many decades, political leaders and experts pushed the EU forward. The EU still seems to be more popular with leaders than ordinary citizens. Some of the "no" votes on the proposed Constitution probably reflected the feeling that the EU was remote from ordinary people. The decision-making institutions of the EU are complex, and many people in the Union do not understand how to influence them. Can people think of themselves as active European citizens sharing a rich European culture and a European political system, or will they resent the EU for being distant, difficult to influence, and a threat to their national way of life and livelihoods?

A girl waves an EU flag while celebrating the organization's fiftieth anniversary. Since its establishment, the EU has changed and grown to a powerful regional organization with 27 participating countries. It has not only fostered peace in Europe, but also created a single economy for its member states, one that would expand with the additional inclusion of members.

## ECONOMIC PROSPERITY

As the problem of war between EU members has receded into the background, the economic aims of the EU have become more important. In 2006, the EU economy as a whole grew at a better rate than the previous few years, and unemployment fell. But for the last 20 or 30 years, prosperity has fallen short of what many leaders have wished.

Two recent major steps to increase growth were adoption of the euro as a common currency and the adoption of the Lisbon Agenda that set the goal for Europe to be a "competitive and dynamic knowledge based economy." Some of the world's best-performing economies are in Europe, while other EU economies are not doing as well. How will the new member-states affect growth and unemployment? Can some countries in the EU maintain a higher level of labor protection and caring services and still grow quickly enough? Will the continued work on a single market make a difference to European growth and prosperity?

The EU is a unique regional organization because it involves the voluntary pooling of national sovereignty to solve common problems. It signals the end of the traditional nation state in Europe. It is an experiment that has turned into an enduring reality. What will the EU look like in another 50 years?

1945    World War II ends.

1950    The Schuman Declaration is made.

1952    The European Coal and Steel Community (ECSC) begins work.

1958    The Treaty of Rome goes into effect, and the European Economic Community (EEC) forms. Belgium, Federal Republic of Germany, France, Italy, Luxembourg, and the Netherlands are members.

1973    Denmark, Ireland, and the United Kingdom join the EEC.

1979    For the first time, citizens of the member states directly elect the European Parliament.

1981    Greece joins the EEC.

1986    Spain and Portugal join the EEC.

1986–1991    The Soviet Union reforms and then dissolves; Communist regimes in Eastern and Central Europe collapse.

1987    Single European Act (SEA) goes into effect.

1993    Treaty of European Union (Maastricht) goes into effect, establishing the European Union (EU). Heads of governments announce the Copenhagen criteria for membership.

1995    Austria, Finland, and Sweden join the EU.

2002    Euro notes and coins are introduced in 12 existing member states.

2004    Czech Republic, Estonia, Cyprus, Latvia, Lithuania, Hungary, Malta, Poland, Slovenia, and Slovakia join

the EU; leaders of member states sign
the new Constitution.

2005    Voters in France and the Netherlands reject the new EU Constitution.

2007    Bulgaria and Romania join the EU; Slovenia joins the euro currency. EU member states sign the Treaty of Lisbon, which incorporates some of the changes laid out in the defeated Constitution.

2008    Cyprus and Malta join the euro currency.

## Chapter 1

1.   European Commission, "Statistical Portrait of the European Union 2007," (Luxembourg: European Communities, 2006).
2.   Ibid., 8.

## Chapter 2

3.   "Consolidated Version of the Treaty Establishing the European Community." Available online at *http://europa.eu.int/eurlex/en/treaties/dat/C_2002325EN.00301.html.*
4.   George Ross, "The EU and Its Policies," *European Politics in Transition*, 5th edition. Mark Kesselman and Joel Krieger, eds. New York: Houghton Mifflin, 2006, p. 93.

## Chapter 3

5.   "Accession Criteria." Available online at *http://ec.europa.eu/enlargement_process/accession_process/criteria/index_en.htm.*
6.   William Horsley, "An Irish Welcome for EU Newcomers," BBC News 1, May 2004. Available online at *http://news.bbc.co.uk/2/hi/europe/3677257.stm.*
7.   Walter Veltroni, "Speech—Signing of the Constitution." Available online at *http://consilium.europa.eu/uedocs/cmsUpload/ENpercent20Veltronipercent20REV.pdf.*

## Chapter 4

8.   Adolf Muschg, "Core Europe: Thoughts About the European Identity," in *Old Europe, New Europe, Core Europe*, Daniel Levy, Max Pensky, John Torpey, eds. London: Verso, 2005, 24.
9.   "Solemn Undertaking Before the Court of Justice by the President and the New Members of the European

Commission," January 21, 2005. Available online at *http://ec.europa.eu/commission_barroso/pdf/oath_en.pdf.*

### Chapter 5

10. International Monetary Fund, World Economic Outlook Database, September 2006. Available online at *http://www.imf.org/external/pubs/ft/weo/2006/02/data/index.aspx.*

11. "Overviews of the European Union Activities: External Trade." Available online at *http://europa.eu/pol/comm/overview_en.htm.*

12. Tobias Buck, "Europe: Services Directive Fails to Win over Companies," *Financial Times*, February 18, 2006. Available online at http://*www.openeurope.org.uk/media-centre/article.apx?newsid=1168.*

13. "Amicus Takes European Services Directive Protest to Strasbourg," February 15, 2006. Available online at *www.amicustheunion.org/Default.aspx?page=3542.*

14. Loukas Tsoukalis, *What Kind of Europe?* (Oxford: Oxford University Press, 2005), 99.

15. "Presidency Conclusions," Lisbon European Council 23, March 24, 2000. Available at *http://www.europarl.europa.eu/summits/lis1_en.htm.*

16. European Commission, "Better off in Europe: How the EU's Single Market Benefits You," (Luxembourg: European Communities, 2005), 6. Available online at *http://ec.europa.eu/publications/booklets/move/56/en.doc.*

### Chapter 6

17. Richard Bernstein, "Europa: Europe's Very Identity at Stake in Farm Talks," *International Herald Tribune*, November 4, 2005. Available online at *http://www.*

*iht.com/bin/print_jpub.php?file=/articles/2005/11/03/ news/europa.php.*

18.  "The Facts of French Food," *Expatica.* Available online at *http://www.expatica.com/actual/article. asp?subchannel_id=61&story_id=1748*; Philip Gordon, "Why the French Love Their Farmers," *YaleGlobal*, November 15, 2005. Available online at *www.yaleglobal. yale.edu/article.print?id=6510.*

19.  Nancy Cochrane, "A Historic Enlargement: 10 Countries Prepare to Join EU," *Amber Waves*, April 2004. Available online at *http://www.ers.usda.gov/Amber-waves/April 04/Features/AhistoricEnlargement.htm.*

## Chapter 7

20.  European Commission, *Europeans and their Languages*, Special Eurobarometer 243 (February 2006). Available online at *http://ec.europa.eu/public_opinion/ archives/ebs/ebs_243_sum_en.pdf.*

## Chapter 8

21.  John McCormick, *Understanding the European Union,* 3rd ed. New York: Palgrave Macmillan, 221–222; International Monetary Fund, World Economic Outlook Database.

22.  "Overview of EU Activities: External Trade," December 2006. Available online at *http://europa.eu/pol/com/ overview_en.htm.*

23.  European Commission, "A World Player—The European Union's External Relations." Available online at *http://www.eurunion.org/globalplayer/worldplayer6. htm.*

24.  "Generalised System of Preferences." Available online at *http://ec.europa.eu/trade/issues/global/gsp/ memo230605_en.htm.*

# BIBLIOGRAPHY

"Accession Criteria." Available online at *http://ec.europa.eu/ enlargement_process/accession_process/criteria/index_en.htm*.

"Amicus Takes European Services Directive Protest to Strasbourg," February 15, 2006. Available online at *http://www. amicustheunion.org/Default.aspx?page=3542*.

Bernstein, Richard. "Europa: Europe's Very Identity at Stake in Farm Talks." *International Herald Tribune*, November 4, 2005. Available online at *http://www.iht.com/bin/print_jpub. php?file=/articles/2005/11/03/news/europa.php*.

Buck, Tobias. "Europe Services Directive Fails to Win over Companies." *Financial Times*, February 18, 2006. Available online at *http://www.openeurope.org.UK/media-centre/article.apx?newsid=1168*.

Cochrane, Nancy. "A Historic Enlargement: 10 Countries Prepare to Join EU." *Amber Waves*, April 2004. Available online at *http://www.ers.usda.gob/Amberwaves/April04/Features/ ahistoricEnlargement.htm*.

"Consolidated Version of the Treaty Establishing the European Community." Available online at *http://europa.eu.int/ eur-lex/en/treaties/dat/C_2002325EN.00301.html*.

"Crop Resistance: Why a Transatlantic Split Persists over Genetically Modified Food." *Financial Times*, February 1, 2006. Available online at *http://pewagbiotech.org/newsroom/ summaries/display.php3?NewsID=988*.

"EU Defeat in Banana Export Battle." BBCNews, August 1, 2005. Available online at *http://news.bbc.co.uk/go/pr/fr/-/2/ hi/business/4735983.stm*.

European Commission. *Better off in Europe: How the EU's Single Market Benefits You*. Luxembourg: European Communities 2005. Available online at *http://ec.europa.eu/publications/booklets/move/56/en.doc*.

———. *Europeans and Their Languages.* Special Eurobarometer 243, February 2006. Available online at http://ec.europa. eu/public_opinion/archives/ebs/ebs_243_sum_en.pdf.

———. *Statistical Portrait of the European Union 2007.* Luxembourg: European Communities, 2006.

———. "A World Player—The European Union's External Relations." Available online at *http://www.eurunion.org/globalplayer/worldplayer6.htm.*

"The Facts of French Food." *Expatica.* Available online at *http://www.expatica.com/actual/article.asp?subchannel_ id=61&story_id=1748.*

"Generalised System of Preferences." Available online at *http:// ec.europa.eu/trade/issues/global/gsp/memo230605_en.htm.*

Gordon, Philip. "Why the French Love Their Farmers." *YaleGlobal,* November 15, 2005. Available online at *http:// yaleglobal.yale.edu/article.print?id=6510.*

Hinrichsen, Don. "On a Slow Trip Back from Hell." *International Wildlife Magazine.* January/February 1998. Available online at *http://www.nwf.org/internationalwildlife/1998/triangle.html.*

Horsley, William. "An Irish Welcome for EU Newcomers." BBC News1, May 2004. Available online at *http://news.bbc. co.uk/2/hi/europe/3677257.stm.*

International Monetary Fund. World Economic Outlook Database. September 2006. Available online at *http://www. imf.org/external/pubs/ft/weo/2006/02/data/index.aspx.*

Lisbon European Council 23 and 24, March 25, 2000. "Presidency Conclusions." Available at *http://www.europarl. europa.eu/summits/lis1_en.htm.*

Maczyk, Henry. "The Black Triangle: Reducing Air Pollution in Central Europe." Available online at *http://www.energy. rochester.edu/pl/blacktriangle/.*

McCormick, John. *Understanding the European Union: A Concise Introduction,* 3rd ed. New York: Palgrave Macmillan, 2005.

"Medical Devices: Regulatory Framework Sound, but Could Be Better Implemented, Says Commission," July 2, 2003. Available online at *http://europa.eu.int/rapid/pressReleasesAction.do?reference=IP/03/934&format=HTML.*

Monnet, Jean. *Memoirs.* Garden City, NY: Doubleday, 1978.

Muschg, Adolf. "Core Europe: Thoughts About the European Identity." In *Old Europe, New Europe, Core Europe.* Edited by Daniel Levy, Max Pensky, John Torpey. London: Verso, 2005.

Osborn, Andrew. "Chocolate War over After 30 Years." *Guardian*, January 17, 2003. Available online at *http://www.guardian.co.uk/food/Story/0,,876571,00.html.*

"Overview of EU Activities: External Trade," December 2006. Available online at *http://europa.eu/pol/comm/overview_en.htm.*

Oxfam. "A Future for Caribbean Bananas." Available online at *http://www.oxfam.org.uk/what_we_do/issues/trade/wto_bananas.htm.*

Ross, George. "The EU and Its Policies." *European Politics in Transition.* 5th ed. Edited by Mark Kesselman and Joel Krieger. New York: Houghton Mifflin, 2006.

"Solemn Undertaking Before the Court of Justice by the President and the New Members of the European Commission." January 21, 2005. Available online at *http://ec.europa.eu/commission_barroso/pdf/oath_en.pdf.*

Tsoukalis, Loukas. *What Kind of Europe?* Oxford: Oxford University Press, 2005.

"United Against the Racists." UEFA.com, January 17, 2006. Available online at *http://www.uefa.com/news/new-sid=385888.htm.*

Veltroni, Walter. "Speech—Signing of the Constitution." Available online at *http://consilium.europa.eu/uedocs/cmsUpload/ENpercent20Veltronipercent20REV.pdf.*

"Written Declaration of the European Parliament on Tackling Racism in Football." December 9, 2005. Available online at *http://www.enar-eu.org/anti-racism-diversity-intergroup/activities/Declaration69_EN.pdf.*

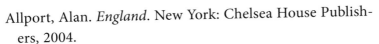

# FURTHER READING

Allport, Alan. *England*. New York: Chelsea House Publishers, 2004.

*The Baltics*. Farmington Hills, Mich.: Lucent Books, 2001.

Bauer, Yehuda. *A History of the Holocaust*. Revised ed. New York: Franklin Watt, 2001.

Blashfield, Jean. *Germany*. New York: Children's Press, 2004.

European Commission Delegation to the United States. *The European Union: A Guide for Americans*. Washington, DC: Delegation of the European Commission to the USA, 2005.

Gay, Kathlyn. *Superfood or Superthreat: The Issue of Genetically Engineered Food*. Berkeley Heights, NJ: Enslow Publishers, 2007.

Jett, Stephen C. *France*. New York: Chelsea House Publishers, 2004.

Lawton, Clive A. *The Story of the Holocaust*. New York: Franklin Watts, 1999.

McCormick, John. *Understanding the European Union: A Concise Introduction*. 3rd ed. New York: Palgrave Macmillan, 2005.

Orr, Tamra. *Slovenia*. New York: Children's Press, 2004.

Shmaefsky, Brian. *Biotech on the Farm and in the Factory*. New York: Chelsea House Publishers, 2005.

Smalley, Mark. *The Rhine*. Austin, TX: Raintree, 1994.

## WEB SITES

European Union
www.europa.eu.int

The link to "Discover the EU" offers many options for reading and viewing data and images. "EU at a Glance" contains basic explanations and information. There are booklets, posters, and maps in the Easy Reading Corner.

European Commission Delegation to the United States
www.eurunion.org

BBC News, Inside Europe
http://news.bbc.co.uk/2/hi/in_depth/europe/2003/inside_europe/
default.stm

# PICTURE CREDITS

**PAGE**

13: © Infobase Publishing

17: © Infobase Publishing

22: Getty Images

25: AP Images

29: © Bettman/Corbis

31: AP Images

39: AP Images

41: © Laszlo Balogh/Corbis

49: AP Images

51: AP Images

60: Mikael Damkier/www.
shutterstock.com

62: AP Images

70: AP Images

73: AP Images

75: AP Images

77: Getty Images

87: AP Images

90: AP Images

92: AP Images

97: AP Images

101: AP Images

107: AP Images

# INDEX

# ABOUT THE CONTRIBUTOR

**PEGGY KAHN** is professor of political science at the University of Michigan-Flint. She teaches courses in European politics, lived in England for many years, and has written about British politics. She has been a social studies volunteer in the Ann Arbor, Michigan, public schools. Her Ph.D. in political science is from the University of California, Berkeley, and her B.A. in history and government are from Oberlin College.

090270

MORRIS AUTOMATED INFORMATION NETWORK

6

341.24    KAHN, PEGGY.
KAH       EUROPEAN UNION.

| | | DATE DUE | | |
|---|---|---|---|---|
| | | | | |
| | | | | |
| | | | | |
| | | | | |
| | | | | |
| | | | | |
| | | | | |
| | | | | |
| | | | | |
| | | | | |
| | | | | |

DOVER TOWN PUBLIC LIBRARY
32 EAST CLINTON ST.
DOVER, NJ 07801